Earth, Air, Fire, and Water

Earth, Air, Fire, and Water

A Memoir of the Sixties and Beyond

MARY SUSANNAH ROBBINS

LEXINGTON BOOKS

A division of
ROWMAN & LITTLEFIELD PUBLISHERS, INC.
Lanham • Boulder • New York • Toronto • Plymouth, UK

LEXINGTON BOOKS

A division of Rowman & Littlefield Publishers, Inc.
A wholly owned subsidiary of The Rowman & Littlefield Publishing Group, Inc.
4501 Forbes Boulevard, Suite 200
Lanham, MD 20706

Estover Road
Plymouth PL6 7PY
United Kingdom

Copyright © 2008 by Lexington Books

All rights reserved. No part of this publication may be reproduced, stored in a retrieval system, or transmitted in any form or by any means, electronic, mechanical, photocopying, recording, or otherwise, without the prior permission of the publisher.

British Library Cataloguing in Publication Information Available

Library of Congress Cataloging-in-Publication Data

Robbins, Mary Susannah, 1946-
  Earth, air, fire, and water : a memoir of the Sixties and beyond / Mary Susannah Robbins.
    p. cm.
  ISBN-13: 978-0-7391-2791-9 (cloth : alk. paper)
  ISBN-10: 0-7391-2791-8 (cloth : alk. paper)
  ISBN-13: 978-0-7391-2792-6 (pbk. : alk. paper)
  ISBN-10: 0-7391-2792-6 (pbk. : alk. paper)
  eISBN-13: 978-0-7391-3050-6
  eISBN-10: 0-7391-3050-1
  1. Robbins, Mary Susannah, 1946- 2. Pacifists—United States—Biography. 3. Women pacifists—United States—Biography. 4. Poets, American—Biography. 5. Women poets, American—Biography. 6. Vermont—Biography. 7. Massachusetts—Biography. I. Title.
  CT275.R716A3 2008
  974.4'04092—dc22
  [B]   2008031239

Printed in the United States of America

To Howard Zinn, for all his kindness and loyalty and encouragement, with all my heart, and to Lawrence Ferlinghetti, whose *A Coney Island of the Mind* was the great revelation of the 1960s for me, with great admiration and thanks for his time, interest, and correspondence.

Some names in this book have been changed for personal reasons.

CONTENTS

	Acknowledgments	ix
1.	Earth and Air and Fire and Water	1
2.	Herbert Robbins	3
3.	Little Hollow	11
4.	The Party	17
5.	Loss	21
6.	Klee	29
7.	Wayne	33
8.	Clio	37
9.	Keith	41
10.	A Question of Style	45
11.	At Home Abroad	49
12.	Hanoi	55
13.	An Electron	63
14.	Debris	67
15.	Why I Love Mistletoe	71
16.	"Miss American Pie"	75
17.	A Matter of Taste	81
18.	You'll Never Be the Same	85
19.	Fish	95
20.	What It Isn't	97
21.	That Night	105
22.	The Last Happy Man	109
23.	Yard Sale	123
24.	"Old Men Should Be Explorers"	125
25.	His Neck	141
26.	Tiananmen Square	143
27.	Thanksgiving	147
28.	Staughton Lynd and Howard Zinn	159
29.	Peace	163
30.	Home	169

ACKNOWLEDGMENTS

"Earth and Air and Fire and Water" was published in the *Larcom Review* under the name of Mary Susannah Robbins.

"Klee" was published in *Colorado North Review* under the pen name of Natalie Berry-Bush.

"At Home Abroad," with some alterations, was published in the *Cool Traveler* under the name of Natalie Berry-Bush.

The concrete poem "Fish" was published in *Phoebus* under the name of Mary Susannah Robbins.

1. EARTH AND AIR AND FIRE AND WATER

Years ago, our place in Vermont was called the old Connolly farm. Pat Connolly owned it and lived there with his twelve sons. He made cider from the apples in the orchard. When Pat wanted to sell the farm, he found a couple who were interested except that they didn't know what they would do with the big old barn down below the house. They said it blocked the view. They went away. That night Pat Connolly's barn burned down. Pat and his twelve sons and the whole town sat and watched. The fire department came too late to save it. Pat brought up all the cider in the cellar and passed it around, and the barn burned to the ground.

And so, in time, the house came into our possession. In the foundations of the old barn grew wild roses, and wild raspberries, and wild blackberries, and a green apple tree, and fireweed. The foundation was a tumble, a tangle of overgrowth, of blossoms and berries and leaves. Things grew there that grew nowhere else. It was a miracle.

The earth in Vermont is like nowhere else. It is warm and grassy and rolling and yellow with sunlight. Indian paintbrushes, vetch, buttercups, Queen Anne's lace, daisies, black-eyed Susans, asters, wild columbine, and a little vermillion flower with a flat stem grow up every summer in the hay fields, and every summer the farmers come with their mowing machines and lay the grass and flowers flat in rows, and then their bailers come and the most satisfying event of the summer occurs: they make the flat swathes into heavy bales which one morning incredibly lie spaced across the field in silence, and the men come with a truck and lift the bales into the truck and drive them away. And then there is stubble, and in the stubble comes up a second crop of flowers, and the hay grows high, and there is a second cutting.

Around the green-golden fields lies wild pasture, steep, rocky little hills and clumps of birch trees and steeplebush and flowers and stone walls and winding paths and toadstools, nooks and crannies of moss and berries and turns in the paths and blue views of distant hills, and, in the dark shade, thousands of raspberries like gold.

The wild pasture grows more and more wild, it grows up to trees, it contains crotches of beauty and pockets of splendor that could only exist in a gnarled, fertile place crisscrossed with walls. Idiosyncratic, twisted, always new, ever more beautiful with the years, its paths reveal glimpses of far heights as beautiful as paintings. It is only to worship, it is only to love, as the hayfields below are just to take to one's breast, breast to breast.

There was water downtown. The river was dammed up every summer for swimming. The water was crystal clear and freezing cold, and minnows and tadpoles swam beside one. One could swim straight toward the dam, and spring aside when the pull got too strong. The water poured over the dam like a natural torrent, not like something made by man. Large trees grew on the banks of the river, and who knew what countries lay around the bend. Dragonflies caught fire, and the brown and gold stone and ooze at the bottom sparkled in the sunlight.

Then they took the dam down in the fall, and the river lay flat and smooth and shallow and thin, and was an altogether different thing. It let one alone. But the next summer it would rise and capture one. One would be half water again, and the fire scintillating all around, and one would exult in freedom once more, and then return, chastened and exhilarated, to the meadows, and peace.

2. HERBERT ROBBINS

When we lived in Chapel Hill, in 1950, we had a gray house with russet shutters, a terrace and a flagstone path. There was a chestnut tree in front and a magnolia tree to the side, and periwinkle around to the back. In back an acre of wild violets held four dogwood trees and a grape arbor. Behind the garage was a garden gone to seed: poppies and marigolds and god knows what all blown in together. Along the driveway was a row of daffodils, and across it was a yard of bluets with a rose bush in the center. Behind our property stood an old tobacco barn. And everywhere there were woods.

We saw a huge terrapin moving very slowly by the side of the road. "He must be a hundred years old," my father said in awe.

An owl in the tree outside my parents' bedroom window hooted all day and slept all night. He could turn his head all the way around. My father tried to shake him down with a stick, but he wouldn't move. "He's mixed up," my father said.

The house was always full of young mathematicians from all over the world. One Indian mathematician used to get so excited that he would chase us children, shrieking with terror and laughter, around the house. My father had to put a stop to it.

"That was a beautiful house," my father reminisced.

When I was six and seven we lived in Princeton. The fall, the bittersweet bushes, the birds' nests in the bare trees seemed to me the most glorious things I could imagine. There were marshes with will o' the wisp and cattails and seedpods and cocoons. My father was a world famous mathematician. He was at the Institute of Advanced Study in 1951–1952.

One day I was having lunch with my father in the cafeteria of the Institute. The large window looked out on the woods behind. The woods were full of birds' nests.

Suddenly my father cried excitedly, "Follow me!" and raced down the corridor. I followed him. Ahead of us I saw what I thought was a cleaning woman: baggy trousers, long white hair. My father caught up to the figure, and it turned to greet us.

"Dr. Einstein," my father said, "I would like you to meet my daughter, Mary Susannah."

A sad, kind face looked down at me.

"Do you like mathematics?" Einstein asked.

While I was trying to answer in the face of so much luminosity, my father intervened.

"She's a literary type," he said.

Afterwards he was jubilant.

"This is wonderful! This is wonderful!" he cried.

***

Now New York was home.

***

Herbert Robbins put down his pencil and looked around his office at the Mathematical Statistics Department at Columbia University with an air of concentrated abstraction. He was responsible, and he was exuberant. He had just solved a problem. He had created it, and he had solved it. His lips puckered absently, and from them came a low whistle. "Gee, whiz!" he said.

G. Whiz entered from his office. G. Whiz was Herbert Robbins's Chinese colleague.

"What do you think?" Herbert Robbins asked G. Whiz, pushing the yellow legal pad across the desk. G. Whiz looked at it. "Gee, whiz," he said.

"Okay," Herbert Robbins smiled. "Gee, whiz," he said, "I've got to get to class." He stood up. He was over six feet, and wore the same wool jacket he had worn in college. It fitted him perfectly. He looked very serious and very funny. "I'm off to be the wizard," he said, and exited.

G. Whiz giggled and went back into his office. After a time I wandered into my father's office. I didn't mind being alone there. I felt most myself in my father's office, whatever city it was in.

I looked around. The same yellow legal pads. The same furniture. The same writing on the blackboard. I glowed. I felt as though all my problems were solved.

The department secretary came in. Miss Patten had known me for years. "How are you," she said. "He'll be out at two."

"Fine," I said. I sat down on the sofa and waited. I picked up the yellow legal pad that my father had shown to G. Whiz. It meant everything to me. I didn't know what it meant, but I absorbed the signs and symbols like nourishment. I had always wanted to be able to speak my father's language.

A door burst open down the hall and I could hear my father laughing and saying, "Okay, okay, okay." Then I heard him whistling down the hall. He burst into the office. I could see that his head was the different shape it always was when he had been teaching, and that he looked like the different person he always looked like after a class.

"What—you?" he said. "Well . . . okay," my father said, "I just have a few things to clear up, and then we'll go out to dinner."

We had dinner at the same old Chinese restaurant. My father always liked the same old things. He had more life to him than anyone I had ever known. He was always the same. He talked to the same old waiters, and they loved him so much. "Who's going to take you out to dinner when I'm gone?" my father asked.

My father was honorable and old fashioned. He was the least deceitful man that I had ever met. Even my mother, even though they were divorced, said that he was "impeccable." "He's outrageous," she said, "but he's impeccable." I found it a relief to be with someone outrageous and impeccable, and funny.

My father was a world famous mathematical statistician. He wrote a book with Harold Courant called *What Is Mathematics?*, higher mathematics for nonmathematicians, which has been translated into scores of languages and is still a classic today. The book was praised by Einstein as "a lucid representation of the fundamental concepts and methods of the whole field of mathematics." My father was politically active. He was one of the first academics to speak out publicly against the war in Vietnam. He went to Harlan County in the 1930s to support the striking miners. He was instrumental in getting a number of Jewish mathematicians and scientists out of the Soviet Union.

"I have very simple wants," he once said to me. I realized that, in the complexity of life in New York, my father was always the same. Complete integrity, like the wool jackets he'd had since college. "Like a good wool suit," he said once when I described a middle-aged acquaintance. "They don't make them like that any more." He was so sweet, and so honest. He tried so hard, and he succeeded. He solved the problem.

One Hallowe'en he came over on his way to a party to show us his costume. He had worn it on the bus down from Columbia. He was wearing a stocking over his head.

The teachers at Brearley, my school, had some of the same qualities as my father, and sometimes my father dated them. They were intelligent, strong-minded, a little odd, and mostly independent. I thought that this was what being grown up was like. When my father said, "I have to go to the orifice," I knew that I had to go to Brearley.

And my mother's friends were the same, simple and not rich, and dignified, and very much individuals. It was this sense of individuals, different characteristics, people each with a certain feeling about them, that I grew up with. Individuals striving, too hard, maybe, or just sitting still. If there was an individual, there was something to love. And all these people seemed to accept their lives, this was just what life was, single or married, professional or doing nothing. It seemed to be simple: you just lived. That was what I hoped.

Sometimes the security of Brearley was stultifying. Sometimes it was cozy and boring and reassuring. There was a time for everything, and everything in its time. There were bells that had rung, songs to be sung, and a wonderful fling to be flung over one's shoulder containing twenty pounds of books at the end of the day, and a long trudge and bus ride and trudge home, and Sara Lee chocolate cake and milk and flinging one's legs over the arm of the armchair to do one's homework in front of the TV that my father had given us. There were three things for dinner: hamburgers and Le Soeur peas, fried chicken, or spaghetti. There was more homework on the edge of one's bed. And then there was something about getting into it and getting out of it and trudging to the bus and trudging up to school.

I loved the edifice that was the school. Its front doors were exciting, its front hall was exciting. In the front hall lurked and poised the Misses Simpson, every one of them in place, who, with hands on the switchboard and the files and the typewriter and the keys and the dismissal cards, would guide the edifice through another day, to its close.

Alison Bradford, Susie Dryfoos, Andra Oakes, all of whose fathers worked for the *New York Times*, were in my class. My mother had known Andra's mother, Marge Hartmann, at Bryn Mawr.

Nina Hirschfeld, Al Hirschfeld's daughter, was in the class above me. We used to look for the Ninas in his drawings.

My father walked into the front hall where I waited for him on Friday afternoons, whistling, his shirtsleeves rolled up, and the little mothers and their little dogs whose nails skittered on the black and white tiles scattered like birds in a fresh breeze. Into stuffy security reality came whistling, straight from class or straight from God knows where, a world outside of this one. I loved it. He was outrageous, but he was impeccable. Security was mean in comparison. "Oh life, life," he would sing out when I least expected it. I knew he was right. I wanted life.

In the catacombs of Brearley the teachers prepared their morning assignments. Eunice Sugar, the Dramatics teacher, sat with her legs apart and her frizzy gray head between her knees, thinking. Livia Fish, the youngest English teacher, put her hand to the huge knob of red brown hair on top of her small white face and smiled a little as she wrote on the blackboard, "Lay a lion limb against me, scan." Livia Fish was very bright and full of surprises. Sarah Poinyard, who taught both English and Dramatics, made a mistake as she wrote out an assignment, and cursed. Kate Quinn, the Mathematics teacher, with her ruddy face and her Scotch plaid kilt with the big safety pin, did nothing at all. C.O. Constable, the History teacher, looking like something between a man and a monkey, shouted a greeting to Kate Quinn as she strode down the hall. Celeste White, the Music teacher for the younger grades, all alone by the piano practiced scales till her triple chins melted into one and she soared out the window and floated on a cloud of talcum powder beyond this lonesome valley to *Jesu Meine Freude*. Stevie, the carpentry teacher, the best of them all, hummed her way into the Shop in her old tweed jacket, and began setting out the hammers, thinking about her thirteen cats. Cherubini Bliss and Giovanni Wax poised in midair, their full lips, full of tones and chords, not quite touching. Cherubini Bliss taught Music to the older girls, seated on the piano with his feet crossed, and Giovanni Wax accompanied him. Louisa Lace spread one of her students' notebooks out on her desk and murmured appreciatively at how many of the words similar in several languages—cavalier, chevalier, caballero; mother, mutter, madre, modar—had as their source "my own head." This girl, Louisa Lace, thought, loved Language. She patted her mauve blouse and adjusted her pale tortoise shell spectacles. She had always been seventy. Antoinette Blanchard, the Supervisor, walked into her office and supervised it from her great height.

All went right that morning.

That afternoon forty seventh graders sat in the Assembly Hall and saw a drop scene drop on Eunice Sugar's head. They watched transfixed as she stood alone on the stage for a moment and then started to cry. She cried as though she could never stop, as though all the injuries, injustices, wrongs, and harms visited through life on Eunice Sugar's head, and nearly asleep, had been shocked awake, and she wept without end, standing in front of forty seventh graders on the stage of the Brearley Assembly Hall, playing her climactic scene, the scene she had been born to play. A chair was brought for her, and she sat with her head in her hands and wept. It seemed to come so easily to her. The forty seventh graders were awestruck. She wept on. They saw the real Eunice Sugar, the great actress, in her greatest role.

When it seemed as though she might never stop, someone led the forty seventh graders out of the Assembly Hall and back to their classroom. The next week Dramatics Class was cancelled. The week after that it met. Eunice Sugar was exactly the same as ever, a little busy, frizzy woman in a pleated skirt. Rehearsals for "H.M.S. Pinafore" went on. Buttercup was as startlingly good as before, and the duet, "Farewell, my own," sung in two twelve year old sopranos, made the seventh graders feel like crying. The stage became a magic place, where girls were boys and children were grownups, and ordinary girls could sing so sweetly that the others shivered and stared. That other scene had been part of Eunice Sugar's life. They had not been supposed to see it. Their frail, sturdy lives transformed themselves into higher and purer notes. That was what it was all about.

I didn't cry about my father and my mother being divorced. Finally one day I was at my father's apartment and my back hurt, and I cried and cried as though I would never stop. "That's natural," said my father. The maid held up a white dress that she had just finished ironing for me. I turned away in a paroxysm of tears. My father motioned to the maid to take it away. "Cry all you want," he said.

My father knew what was natural.

I loved flowers and plants. I always thought that the earth, the dark earth at the bottom of the plants, was my father. Deepest, darkest love, deepest darkest loss. My room looked like a plant

Chapter 2

nursery. Among African violence, woe begonias, terrapins, sweetish ivy, Phil O'Dendron, Rhoda Dendron, and spite her plants, I dreamed of a lovely fuchsia. In the middle of the table was a bunch of everlasting from my father, with a note, which he had sent me after he had read part of this book. The note read,

> I have here only made a nosegay of culled flowers, and have brought nothing of my own but the thread that ties them together.
>
> Michel Eyquem de Montaigne
> 1553–1592

My father had an Adolph Dehn print on his wall. It showed a man selling balloons under a bombed out wall, and it was called "Always Tomorrow."

My father had read everything and remembered everything. He had heard all the music and could whistle it. He knew lots of famous people. He knew lots of people whom no one had ever heard of. He knew. One day he said to me excitedly, as though he had just solved an important problem, "I think everything is impossible!" Everything was impossible and anything was possible. My mother and my father's colleagues told me over and over of the time a colleague had solved a problem and came in great excitement to my father and cried, "I wonder what Gauss will say to me when I meet him in Heaven!" and my father had said joyfully, "He'll say, 'Have you seen Robbins lately?'"

3. LITTLE HOLLOW

I arrived at Little Hollow, a progressive boarding school in southern Vermont, in September of 1961. My mother and my sister Mistletoe helped me unpack, and then they left. I stood in line for the barbecue by the dining hall, looking across at the mountains. These mountains, stark and brilliant, were nothing like the rolling foot hills of Randolph. I felt the ties, myself, my heart, break. The great continuum of my mother moved off like a cumulus cloud. I was outlined in loss. I had no story. For the first time in my educational life, boys all around me. It was like having no father.

I cried in the southern Vermont woods for days. Once I looked up and saw two girls on horseback pass on the path below me, each with her hair in a knot, bitter, sexual, severely disciplined. They knew the secret, had given up childhood, held the bit firmly, sat up straight, passed by in silence.

I knew I couldn't go back to Brearley, even if I wanted to. I sat in the library and stared at the spine that pronounced in large letters, "YOU CAN'T GO HOME AGAIN." Some tie had broken. If I went back something terrible would happen. I would fall apart.

I made friends.

The center of social life for my "clique"—that's what they were called, only somewhat facetiously—at boarding school in Vermont was not the Social Room, which was usually empty save for Carol Simmons spinning around alone to the record player, nor was it the Formal Garden, where juniors and seniors were allowed two cigarettes after dinner. We sophomores, and a couple of freshmen, could have all the cigarettes we wanted, whenever we wanted, at the PTA.

The Pine Tree Association had been started by those underclassmen who saw no reason why juniors and seniors should be the only ones allowed to smoke, and indeed saw no reason for most of the rules at Little Hollow. Little Hollow was a mixture of Puritanism and Communism. We'd been told that when it was founded there had been a rule that you couldn't hold hands with the same person in public two nights in a row; it was individualism, and not good for the community. And salt and pepper had been banned as luxuries. You *had* to ski four afternoons a week. The founder's daughter was a physicist who gave the A bomb to China. Little Hollow's Communist Chinese student, David Kuo, would go down the ski hill out of control, ski poles waving, shouting, "God damn Amelica! God damn Little Hollow! God damn Amelican capitalist system!"

The year before I came, a few juniors and seniors had been expelled for that most forbidden of crimes, sleeping together. Their sleeping bags had been found in the woods, with their nametags on them, and they were now living happily in New York. They were gods. The names on those nametags were known even to the freshmen. They were our ideals, our models, and we became the new models. Our class was Little Hollow's nightmare.

But it was early, and we were still very young. Whenever we had a free moment, we went down the path behind the dorms, into the woods, and through the trees to where a green door propped against a juniper formed the entrance to the PTA. Beyond the door pine needles lay in a wide circle around the Pine Tree itself, and someone was always there, puffing away.

Most of the people in my clique were boys, and I carried on a series of courtships at the PTA that rarely progressed beyond the smoking stage. It was a place to pour out real or imagined agonies, and sometimes the end of a whiskey bottle. It was a place not to be caught in: smoking, and certainly drinking, meant expulsion for us. During my years at Little Hollow, all but one of my friends were suspended or expelled. I escaped a like fate by going to Radcliffe from my junior year.

It was all so new to me—smoking, boys, sex, drinking, adolescence, homesickness, and the unknown miasma, drugs—that I hid my monumental confusion behind an appearance of such calm and control that most of my friends thought of me, quite naturally, as their mother, and the romances that happened to girls who lost their minds over things never happened to me. When romance did happen to me, I lost my mind completely.

In the meantime we slept, ate, and worked. I learned enough Russian to read Yevtoshenko and Lermontov. I felt as though I had come home. When I went to Radcliffe I wanted to study Russian literature and the Russian Revolution, but by then coming home had turned elusive. I spent half a year in a Russian tutorial on "The Song of Igor's Campaign," then switched into English. I am writing in English now.

This was the early 1960s. The great night of the PTA was the night of the Cuban missile crisis. The Cuban missile crisis was the closest we ever came to having a nuclear war with the Soviet Union. The whole school gathered in the assembly hall to listen to the radio. Afterwards, we were each allowed one phone call. I called my mother and wished her goodbye, and she laughed and said, "See you in Heaven." And then our clique went down to the PTA and lay on the pine needles watching the sky. There was said to be a missile base off to the north. We talked of death. We were very excited. One boy, braver than the rest, put his hand on my thigh. Love and death were too much for me. I cried out. Everyone looked nonplussed, disappointed. We trailed back up the path to the school in the dark.

It was in the infirmary that I got to know Rick.

One night I awakened, in my upper bunk in the room I shared with three other girls, raging with fever, aching all over. Our dorm head drove me through the freezing night to the infirmary. I fell into bed and slept for days. When I woke up and cautiously emerged from my room, Jack had moved into the room next to me with the same bug. I spent the next two weeks recuperating in

Jack's room, where the head nurse moved me to make my room free for an even sicker boy. It was an epidemic of the dreaded Little Hollow crud.

Jack would lie on his bed and I would lie on mine, both of us fully dressed, and talk and talk. Jack was writing a novel. Part of each day he would write, and part of each day he would read me what he had written. He ran out of paper, and the head nurse supplied him with old envelopes. He decided to make the back of an envelope his medium. He was very excited about this. He would come to the end of an envelope back, and that would be the end of a section. Then he would cover another envelope back. I remember his saying defiantly, "Why *shouldn't* the back of an envelope be the medium?"

When we were no longer considered contagious, Rick came up to see us. Rick was Jack's best friend. He sat on the edge of Jack's bed, a visitor from the strange, icy, wildly lonely world of classes and work jobs and sports that we were safe from here for a while, tucked into our literary life. "I'd do anything to get in here," Rick said. He came every day. He told us the snow outside was six feet deep. I didn't know how I would ever go back out.

Jack would talk about how we'd take over the *New Yorker* when we got out of school. Rick would talk about flying model airplanes. He and a friend used to fly them together at home. "It goes up, and it loops the loop, and then it goes smash," he told us. "Wouldn't it be great to fly a real airplane? I'd take you up in it," he said to me. "We could fly, and then we'd lean over the side and puke. . . ." He was kind to me. He knew I didn't have a clue.

Rick got kicked out of Little Hollow in the spring. One day he refused to get up for Morning Barn. Morning Barn was the Test of Character to end all Tests of Character at Little Hollow. Little Hollow was very big on Character. Morning Barn meant that you got up at 4 a.m. and put on your dung caked blue jeans and walked half a mile in a blizzard to the barn and shoveled shit for two hours. You had to do it or you wouldn't graduate. We used to say that we'd pay the price of tuition *not* to go to Little Hollow. But once

Rick said, "You kids are in Heaven and you don't know it." He said, "I feel as though I don't deserve to be here." So one morning Rick just stayed in bed, and the guy who was head of the barn appeared in his doorway and nearly killed him, and then all the seniors in his dorm beat him up, and then he went home.

Little Hollow changed its admissions policy. It stopped taking crazy geniuses from New York whom it thought it could encourage with fresh air and potato picking. For a while it took only prepubic chemists. Gradually it found its norm. We only found one another.

Being kicked out of Little Hollow was the end of Rick's bearable life. When I knew him for the next few years, in New York, he was trying to write on no money and on drugs, and it got worse. It got worse for me, too, even though I went to college a year early.

I was hysterical when I heard that Rick was leaving. He wouldn't speak to me. He was packing. I found our English teacher in the greenhouse, watering the geraniums. "Is there anything I can do?" I asked. "Nooo . . ." he said, "nothing. There's nothing anyone can do. Just stay away from him."

There was nothing I could do. Everything had happened. All the rest was aftermath.

That spring Rick had taken my hand one night and run with me down the library lawn to the music shack. We sat there in the dark. I couldn't breathe. I said, "I love you." There was silence. Then Rick said, "For a minute I almost believed you."

One day we had been alone together in the English room and I lay down on the table. Rick smiled, the most beguiling smile, and looked down at me. Then he walked out the door, saying, "Stay like that. That's how I like you." Adulthood started, my smile that would never be the same. I stayed like that forever. He didn't come back.

4. THE PARTY

That summer, Carol Simmons, a close, fée friend of mine from Little Hollow, had a coming out party.

Rick wasn't invited.

I saw him all the time in New York. He was writing and starving in a room on the West Side.

I was in love with him.

The party was to be on Carol's family's estate outside New York. There would be a band under a canopy, and a champagne breakfast at dawn.

My mother took me to Lord and Taylor's and we bought my first formal dress. It was cream colored brocade, very fitted. Rick loved it.

Jack and Terry, with rented tuxedos, and I took the train from Penn Station. My mother said that we were like the Marx brothers going to see Margaret Dumont. We were met by the Simmons' chauffeur.

I had been to Carol's place once before. It was awfully disorienting. Her father had a bomb shelter in the enormous back yard. People were afraid of a nuclear attack from the Soviet Union in those days, and if you were extremely wealthy you could have your own private bomb shelter built underground of cement, stocked with enough canned food and water so that you would presumably survive until the attack was over and the radioactive fallout had cleared. Then you could come out and see if anyone else had survived.

Carol's father was the Director of *Time-Life*. Her parents hovered on the landing with silent little smiles.

Some of the girls were to sleep in one of the bedrooms, and some were to sleep in the porch off of it.

I felt sick.

The afternoon dragged along. Eventually we got into our clothes. I thought I might not go to the party. I said hysterically that I was going to stay in the bedroom. Everyone was a little hysterical.

In some far off bedroom Carol was getting dressed.

I went. There was a canopy, and the band, and champagne, and a swimming pool. I sat at a table and got very drunk. I wandered down a path in the shrubbery, terribly happy in my new dress. When I came back and sat down, Carol's brother Smitty introduced himself to me.

Carol had talked about nothing except how much she loved Smitty all year. Aglow with champagne, I leaned toward him and told him so. He was amazed. "I had no idea," he said.

We danced. Then he left me. The dark night dragged on to the sounds of the band and the insects.

I went up to the porch and went to sleep.

At noon the next day there was lunch on the lawn. I was very hung over, and my nerves were screaming. There *had* been a champagne breakfast, and some people had gone swimming in their clothes. I couldn't imagine how anyone could have lasted.

I was sitting by the bomb shelter eating a plateful of chicken salad when Carol came up to me with a white, stony face.

"You *betrayed* me," she said.

This seemed to be what people, even Rick, said to me in those days, when everyone thought I was God.

"What?" I said.

"You *betrayed* me," she said again. "You told Smitty that I loved him."

I looked at her in amazement. I hadn't imagined a family that didn't say that sort of thing to one another. I thought of the bomb shelter and the parents with their silent smiles.

I flung the plate of chicken salad across the lawn. It landed on the bomb shelter.

"*Leave me alone!*" I yelled. I ran up the stairs and out onto the sleeping porch.

I fell on my bed and howled.

Carol Simmons came upstairs. She sat on the edge of the bed.

"The truth isn't in me, Nan," she said.

I thought that that was a very good way of putting it.

"I'm going *home*," I said. Where's Rick? I thought desperately.

I got the timetable from the bedroom. There was a train in half an hour.

"I can just make it," I said. I wasn't sure I could.

"If you're going, we're going, too," everyone said.

"Oh, please stay," everyone said.

It would have been too painful to go.

I washed my face and combed my hair and went downstairs, and we all sat around the bomb shelter under the trees.

5. LOSS

Rick and Terry and I were sitting around in the living room in our house in Randolph the summer after Rick had been kicked out of Little Hollow.

Rick said, "Life is a great white light shining me in the eyes."

He had apprenticed himself to a piano tuner, Boris Ostravsky. We had a tuning fork, and he used to tap it and laugh.

Rick said, "My burning ambition is to commit suicide."

Terry's mother had died the year before, and he couldn't get over it.

"Death is amazing," he said

"Death isn't amazing," said Rick. "It's life that's amazing."

In our apartment at 80th and Madison, Rick had suddenly started screaming at me, "You're a machine! Press a button and out comes love!" It was because of Terry. I had said to Rick, "I love you, but I'm not in love with you." He was not as conventionally attractive as Terry, and I thought that this was true.

Rick said, "That's like saying, 'Yes, but no.'"

He ran out the door and down the four flights of stairs. I ran out the door and down the stairs after him. I heard the front door slam.

Chapter 5

I collapsed on the stairs and burst into tears. I had never cried like that. I had no idea why I felt the way I did.

When I went back up to the apartment, Mistletoe said, "You're too good."

"No," I said, "that's not it."

Rick used to sit in the gooseneck rocker that had belonged to my grandmother's aunt and mimic Kipling's elephant child whose trunk was being pulled, "Led go. You're hurtig be," and laugh.

He said to me, "You have a heart like a block of ice."

I was sitting in the armchair one evening and he came and knelt down in front of me and buried his face in my skirt.

Once when he was leaving the apartment, Rick jumped over the railing of the stairs and onto the flight below. I was terrified. Once in Randolph we were playing ball and the ball got caught on the roof. Rick climbed up to get the ball, and he jumped off the roof.

He was always jumping off things.

We had an apartment on the fourth floor of a brownstone at the corner of 80th street and Madison Avenue. The fuse box for the apartment, to my mother's delight, was labeled "Mrs. Huntington's Library" Outside the huge wavy glass living room windows we could see, in one block, the Food O Mart, the tiny Great Atlantic and Pacific Tea Company, the florist, the furrier, and the Rhinelander Pharmacy. Directly across the street was the hardware store, and above it the Kraushaar Gallery, which had abstract expressionist paintings in its windows.

All the kids from Little Hollow used to spend their vacations there. It was called "the pad." My mother was always extremely generous to young people, and none of these kids wanted to go home. It was the same when we moved to Cambridge. All the Harvard and Radcliffe students congregated on our living room sofa.

In Cambridge my mother was great friends with Kathleen Kennedy Townsend and with Benjy Goodman, Benny Goodman's daughter.

One night in the apartment in New York I was standing by the piano and Rick suddenly yelled, "Gangway! I'm going to commit suicide!" And he rushed past me and leapt out the window.

I was frozen in horror. Then I screamed, "Mummy! Rick just jumped out the window!"

My mother came tearing in. "*What!*" she said.

Rick had caught himself with his hands on the windowsill and was dangling four floors above the street.

"*Press on his hands!*" said my mother. "*So he can't let go!*"

I pressed my hands down on his fingers with all my might.

"Let go," said Rick, "so I can pull myself up."

Very reluctantly I let go.

He pulled himself up and in through the window.

"Why did you do that?" he said, flexing his hands. "You could have broken my fingers."

My mother was absolutely furious.

"Listen, Rick," she said, "I'm never going to let you in this house again unless you make me a solemn promise *never, never, never* to do *any* such thing *ever* again."

Rick looked abashed. "I promise," he said.

"*Swear* to it." said my mother.

Rick said, "I swear."

My mother turned around and put her hands to her head.

"I give up," she said, and walked away.

Rick was working as a stock boy in a store, pushing racks around. He said to me, "You don't know what life is like." He was living in the warehouse district on West Thirty-eighth Street and writing a novel. It was winter. Rick was at our apartment and it was midnight and he couldn't leave. He would go to the door and then come back, and then go to the door and come back.

Chapter 5

Suddenly I couldn't stand it any more. I couldn't stand any more destruction or any more conflict. My father had forbidden all of us to see him now that he was on drugs."

"*Get out!*" I said. "*Get out and never come back.*"

He told me the next day that he had spent the night in a snow bank, and that two boys had said to him, because his hair was long, "Are you a boy or a girl?"

When Lincoln Center first opened, Terry and I got tickets. Both of us and Rick rode down in a taxi, me between them,

"Poor Susannah," Rick said.

Terry and I rode up the escalator. Rick was standing at the bottom, looking up after us.

I must have left my heart with Rick at that moment. I felt as though I were going completely insane as Terry and I stood in the glass foyer outside the concert hall. I don't remember the concert at all, but when I was alone with Terry in the intermission, I felt as thought there were rockets going through my head. Terry went to get some champagne.

The summer before I went to Radcliffe, Rick came up to Randolph. He was on drugs and he was writing a novel. "You have to be able to walk away from it," he said. He spent all day typing in the little room off of the porch. He showed me part of it. It was about his psychiatrist. "You're a paid pal," Rick had said to him.

Rick was lying on the chaise lounge on the porch. He had a pipe and he had some hash and he had some tin foil and he had some matches. He asked me to bring him a pin to make holes in the tinfoil so that he could put it over the pipe and smoke the hash.

I did, and I felt terrible. I felt my complicity in his taking drugs. I felt weak, and I had never felt that way before.

At Little Hollow Rick had told me that his parents had put him in mental hospitals when he was a child. "The people there were freaks," he said. "They had two heads." He had told me that his most recent psychiatrist had shot himself and his dog. It was a Scottie.

Rick was much more grown up than all of us at Little Hollow, and he was a very good, affectionate person. He spouted Shakespeare and Joyce and was very funny about them, and he was a fantastic pianist. He said about Terry, whom I was always trying to get to love me and who was beside himself about the loss of his mother, "He takes you for granite."

Rick and I were lying on one of the beds on the porch one night. I was lying on top of him and on top of the blanket. He kissed me. "You have a beautiful mouth," he said.

Then he pulled the blanket over his head. I couldn't stand that suddenly he wasn't there. I pounded with my fists on the blanket.

I had thought I loved Terry. He played classical guitar and it was wonderful. But my feelings for Rick were a volcano.

Anyway, one night Rick picked up a rifle that had stood in the corner of the living room since we had bought the house. No one had ever paid any attention to it and no one knew if it was loaded. Rick aimed it at me.

He stood there for what seemed like a long time, long enough for me to look down the barrel and into infinity.

He pulled the trigger.

It wasn't loaded.

Rick and I were sleeping on the porch.
He said, "I need each other."
He made a flying leap and landed in my bed.
He laughed.
"It's bigger than both of us," he said.
I said, "I can't live without you."
"I'd be afraid to say that," he said.

I woke up in the morning and Rick was gone. There was just a space on the grass where his car had been.

He was very fond of my mother, and I think in part he was ashamed to have taken advantage of her hospitality.

I knew I was pregnant.
I stood on the porch looking out at the trees.
It was the greatest loss of my life.

I miscarried in the second month.

The fall that I went to Radcliffe, I came down to New York to spend Thanksgiving vacation with my father. Rick came over. He sat at the kitchen table; he put his head in his hands. He said, "Marry me."
 I couldn't say anything. I was somewhere else by then.
 My father forbade me to see Rick, but we used to get in his car and just drive around Central Park, not talking.
 I was madly in love.

I took a poetry writing seminar that year with Stephen Sandy. I went to his rooms for an interview. I wore the yellow and orange flowered dress that had made Rick say, "She looks happy, but she isn't," so affectionately. No matter how conflicted Rick was about me, I thought that he was the only person who had ever understood how I felt about anything. That's enough to make you love and trust someone, isn't it? I trusted Steve Sandy in the same way that I had trusted Rick, and years later, when I had published a book of poems, I called him up.
 "*I* remember you," he said thoughtfully.
 I asked him if I could send him *Amelie*, and he said yes.
 I ran into him shortly after that in Harvard Square. "It's a wonderful book," he said.
 I called him later, to ask him if he would write a cover comment for a second edition, saying exactly that. His wife answered the phone.
 "Would you ask him if I could talk to him?" I said. "Tell him he's the only poet I trust."
 She laughed.

"I'll tell him," she said.
He wrote the comment.

My father came to visit me at Radcliffe, and he came to one of my classes, Poetics, taught by Robert Fitzgerald. Fitzgerald was talking about John Berryman. He said, "He could turn on a dime, like that football player—what was his name?"

"Albie Booth," my father said from the back of the room.

"Yes," said Robert Fitzgerald, immediately warm and attentive. He had been looking vaguely out of the window. "Albie Booth."

My father was ecstatic.

"I didn't go into English Literature," my father said to me later, "because I didn't want to *read* "Kublai Kahn," I wanted to *write* it."

When I had been accepted at Radcliffe, my father wanted to introduce me to Jacques Barzun's daughter, Isabelle, who would be in my class. The four of us met at the faculty club for lunch. Isabelle and I couldn't think of a thing to say to each other, so Jacques Barzun said, "I just learned a very interesting game," and he taught us how to play 'honky tonky donkey,' the game in which you say, "Ridiculous horse," and everyone has to guess, "Silly filly." We played it all during lunch. As my father and I left Butler Hall, my father was silent for a moment, and then he said, "Angry fish."

"I don't know," I said.

He said, "Mad shad."

The main thing about both my father and my mother is that they were terribly intelligent and honest and funny, and the same has been true of all of the men I have loved. We just laughed. That was what kept us going. When they lost their sense of humor, they died. My father died, but he didn't lose his sense of humor.

Chapter 5

Long after I had graduated, my father came up to visit me in Cambridge during a Harvard-Radcliffe reunion. We went together, and we ran into his friend Meyer Schapiro, the Marxist art historian. My father introduced us and then left us alone together.

"You look exactly like your father," Meyer Schapiro said. "There's no doubt whose daughter *you* are."

"I don't think that's a very nice thing to say," my father said when I told him this.

"I think it's a *very* nice thing to say," I said.

My father was a very faithful person. "The wife you save may be your own!" he said to me once laughingly.

"Meyer Schapiro has the most beautiful face I've ever seen," I said. My father smiled and nodded.

My father's mind had the clarity and distance of a mathematician's or a scientist's, and when I talked to him it was contagious.

"I thought of a joke," I said to him once. "Why do so many people go into mathematics?"

"I don't know," he said thoughtfully.

"Because there is safety in numbers."

"Heavens!" he said.

Once when I was having a show at a café I ran into the physicist Victor Weisskopf.

"Do you know my father, Herbert Robbins?" I asked.

"Oh, yes," he said. "I know who he is. You're in a hard position."

"He knew who I was?" asked my father, completely thrilled.

Victor Weisskopf fell in love with a painting, and I gave it to him. It was one of my best paintings. He told me he had Picassos and Mattises all over his walls that he had bought for nothing when the artists were very young, and he wrote to me that he had hung my painting among them.

6. KLEE

I went away to Radcliffe from my junior year in the fall of 1963. My mother and my younger sister Mistletoe left New York as well and moved into an apartment a block from my dorm. We had lunch with Rick at Horn and Hardart's in New York—his father had given him a credit card for Horn and Hardart's—and then we got in a taxi for the airport. As I got into the taxi I felt as though I was leaving half of myself in New York.

In college my favorite painting was one by Klee called "Ad Parnassum." It is made up of squares of misty colors, all tending upward toward the empyrean. I was in love with Rick, and desperately homesick, and that painting was where I wanted to go.

Rick was on drugs in New York, and I hardly ever saw him any more. The last time had been the Christmas vacation I spent at my father's, when one evening Terry had called me and said, "Rick is very sick," and to come and bring some aspirin. I lied to my father that I was going over to Terry's, that, yes, his parents would be there, and I went to the drugstore and asked for the largest bottle of aspirin they had and took a taxi down to West 38th Street.

I'd never been to Rick's room. It was on the second floor. The bathroom was down the hall. The room was tiny and almost filled by Rick's bed and a Steinway grand that his parents had given him. A Steinway grand, in that place. I squeezed in the door. Rick was lying in his pajamas on the bed, wrapped up in a blanket, saying,

"I'm so cold. I'm so cold." "What did he take?" I asked Terry. "Vitamin B," Terry said. The needle lay on the bed.

"Here's the aspirin," I said. Rick got up and went down the hall to the bathroom to take two.

He came back and lay on the bed. He was shaking. I started to walk around the grand piano, as far around it as I could get, and back, and around, and back. I felt nothing, except that I might explode. I felt as though I were acting. I got on the bed and rubbed Rick's back. There was a print of a Northern Renaissance painting over the head of the bed. Rick knelt in his pajamas and looked at the painting in silence. He looked at the infinitely sad, blue horizon that all those paintings have. "I can't *get* there," he said.

I felt as though I could get to Parnassus by looking at the Klee. It was easy.

When I first read *Catch-22* and I got to the part where Snowden is shot and he keeps saying, "I'm so cold. I'm so cold," and they can't figure out what's wrong with him and finally they see that his stomach's blown open and they can see the stewed tomatoes he had for lunch, it took me a while to think what it reminded me of. But I got there.

Rick died, but not that time, and not that way. But that's my Breughel: Rick kneeling in his pajamas in front of a painting, saying, "I can't get there."

When I first left Rick in New York and came to college, I used to go out every morning and walk around the neighborhoods watching the sun come up. I wrote a poem doing this one morning. It went like this:

The New Wife

Never to walk and wonder high in the heart's hunting,
Fearing the soul's constriction, the sight of a seed,
Seeking through endless mornings the gold sky,
In the glass of others' houses are suns that burn.
Now to contain the longing, heaven and earth,
Seas of mist in a drop of water running and spilled,

Feeling through waving branches a new wind
Flap the calm sheets endlessly. Night must fall.
Sunset and sunrise now are no moments to go
Uncaptured on the breath of the changing world, but see,
Low in the low land, close in the dark,
Moon in a mirror while the room sleeps, filled and
                                                    dreaming.

Safe in my room at college one morning, my roommate busy at the mirror, I wrote:

Soon she would move from the window,
Once more to feed the child.
She brandished the day like a glass.
Only her dreams were wild.
She stepped, and new trees arose.
She bent, and her hands ploughed wide
Furrows of sun in the earth.
She declined to pick the rose
That was day. The day declined.
The flower rose, rose, fell,
Petal and leaf, to the wind.
"But it falls untouched," she cried.
"I will not help its death.
"I will help no one's death."

The child cried. The woman turned,
Bewildered. Outside, the day
Sounded its golden clang.
Frightened, she turned away.
Dark brilliance and ice fell back.
Behind the flowered screen,
Breath, and she breathed again.

It has not changed. And these stories are a way of seeing what is there, what was always there.

7. WAYNE

Everybody of my generation at some point or another always asks each other, "Where were *you* on November 22, 1963?" I was in the dorm. I had just washed my hair, and I had come out of the shower and was sitting on the top bunk in my room, in a bathrobe, about to dry it. The dorm was nearly empty, since it was early afternoon, and I heard a radio playing down the hall, but it sounded like news, not music, and I heard people talking. I decided to go and investigate. I got down from the top bunk and padded down the hall in my bare feet. Some people were gathered in someone's room, and there was the radio. "What's going on?" I asked. "President Kennedy's been shot," someone said. I laughed. I thought she was making a joke.

It wasn't a joke. He was shot and killed riding in a motorcade in Dallas, Texas. Vice President Lyndon Johnson was sworn in as president immediately.

I went back to the top bunk and lay there with my wet hair. I lay there for a long time. In the evening I called my new boyfriend, Wayne. He came over and we went to the Square. The street was mobbed with silent people just standing around as though they were waiting for something, and the blare of radios. We walked back across the Common. I felt incredibly fragile, as if the sky had been torn away and anything could come in. Wayne didn't talk. I said, "We're open to the skies."

Chapter 7

Wayne was the brother of a girl I'd been at Little Hollow with, and a physics section man. That seemed like a professor to me. Wayne was a junior.

Since Little Hollow had been in the country, I had never gone out with a guy who wore ironed shirts, tweed jackets, and topcoats. I felt as though I'd never even *seen* one. I fell in love with all these things, and with the way his shirts smelled of buttered toast. Maybe this was because we ended our evenings at a cafeteria, Albiani's, eating English muffins and trying to figure out what to make of us. In his suite I discovered sex, or some of it.

Many years later I ran into Professor Mayberry-Lewis, who had been the Master of Adams House when I knew Wayne, and his wife at a cocktail party. We were talking and laughing and I mentioned Wayne and "parietals," the hours beyond which no woman was allowed in Harvard men's rooms.

"I was supposed to be sure that they were kept to," Professor Mayberry-Lewis said. "My wife thought I should, but I didn't think it was any of my business."

He looked at me and smiled. "It's nice to meet you after all these years," he said.

All the Radcliffe women used to gather with their dates on the porch of the dorm before curfew, but Wayne was a private type. We always stopped in the shadows at a telephone pole before the corner. Wayne would lean up against it and take me in his arms.

The blond men in my life all have been stable and, in some way deeply rooted in their personalities, if not in their politics, conservative. I needed a blond, conservative, butter and toast guy right then. Kennedy was dead, and dark Rick was on drugs.

I couldn't talk to Wayne, we could only be close physically, and I felt split in two. In my mind I was clinging desperately to him, but outwardly I must have seemed indifferent. Wayne had no experience in trying to make someone talk, and no perception of the turmoil I was going through. After we came back from our Christmas vacations, mine spent in New York with and without Rick and completely unbearable, Wayne said to me, "I didn't miss you as much as I thought I would." "Were you surprised?" I asked, watching my life drifting away. Wayne said, "Look, I like—hell, I *love* you physically, but I don't love you emotionally," and that was it.

No more phone calls, no more English muffins. I'd never formally "gone out" with anyone before, so I'd never formally "broken up" with anyone. Relationships at boarding school were a lot more informal, if not more casual. I had a lot of trouble with "the dating scene" after having milked cows with boys at 4 a.m. I didn't understand why Wayne and I could never see each other again, as though we were space ships going in opposite directions.

In "The Enterprise of Science," my favorite course, we were discussing the effect of the invention of the telescope on seventeenth century poetry. Wayne's cheek and his soft neck seemed like a new planet that had swum into my ken. I could still see them, so close. But they were as if seen through the wrong end of a telescope now, far off, unreachable. I had discovered them—they were mine. I could hardly bring myself to go to class because it meant that I had to look down at the backs of thirty rows of men students' necks.

We had all watched Kennedy's funeral in the dorm living room. There was Jackie, who always looked the same no matter what, and there were the children, who, I knew, had been told, "Kennedys don't cry." I had never seen so much black.

The future had been cut off in an instant, and no one knew what would happen next. Whatever you think of Kennedy, at that time there had seemed something sure about him. That sureness went out of American life for good.

Kennedy's death was a personal loss, like the loss of Rick, like the loss of Wayne. It changed people's personal lives.

8. CLIO

Clio roomed on the second floor of my dorm at Radcliffe. I roomed on the third. Clio and her boyfriend Kelly Cohn spent most of their time in the living room on the first floor.

It was 1964.

Clio was a playwright. She had plays performed at the Ex, the college experimental theatre. She was a very good writer. She wrote an absurdist play about the maids in the dorm kitchen. She didn't know how brilliant she was.

Clio was very beautiful. She had black hair and long blue eyes with black lashes, a strong nose, and a way of looking at you out of the corners of her eyes and giggling hysterically that undid the noble, classical effect. Kelly Cohn was slight and shaggy and wild-eyed. Clio and Kelly Cohn were like a couple of kids. They laughed and fought and he played the harmonica in the living room. Kelly Cohn reminded me of Bob Dylan. He also reminded me of a lot of things I had lost, like Rick. But I didn't realize that. I just knew that I had a strong, black feeling in my heart about him. I don't think I spoke to him more than once.

Clio wore black tights and black skirts and olive green sweaters. But we were not beatniks or hippies at college. Clio was from a wealthy family in Rhode Island. She was shy, for all her laughter. She drifted around, for all her strength. She would go down to the shore and listen to the conversation of men in bars, to get material.

But on the whole she was attached to Kelly Cohn, and she stayed in the living room with him.

Clio and Thalia were friends. They were the free spirits in the dorm. Thalia had the opposite coloring to Clio. She had fair straight hair and very white skin. She was tall, and she stooped. When I think of *She Stoops to Conquer*, I think of Thalia, stooping. But Thalia wasn't interested in conquering anything. She drifted around the dorm in her nightgown, murmuring to herself, Spenser held up to her nearsighted eyes with one hand, something to eat in the other. Everyone loved Thalia. She was very sweet natured, responsive, and she laughed a lot. She and Clio giggled together. Everyone teased Thalia. You couldn't help it. She laughed so hard when you did.

Clio and Thalia were a lot like me, and comforting to have around. Clio embraced the 1960s and made the best of things. Thalia retreated into nocturnal habits and made the best of things.

The Vietnam War threatened to kill us all. I knew that. I went to Washington to demonstrations. My mother and Mistletoe and I went to hear Martin Luther King speak in Boston. I took a course from Hilary Putnam, who was, I believe, the only professor to support the student strike.

Clio and Kelly Cohn broke up. Clio met a guy who was completely different from Kelly Cohn. He was in SDS and he became one of the leaders of the Harvard strike in 1968.

SDS, Students for a Democratic Society, was a campus-based left wing organization which opposed the Vietnam War and the draft and which believed that students should try to form a coalition with the working class.

I went out with Keith, who, when I met him, was totally unpolitical. He wanted to escape from adolescence and become a priest. By the time we broke up he had been radicalized. He joined Clio's boyfriend and SDS in the strike.

The strike is history. The students took over the administration building. The administration called the police to remove the students. The police wore riot gear and wielded truncheons. That is an unforgettable sight.

Clio's boyfriend was expelled. He and Clio got married. He was drafted. He decided to go rather than seek a deferment because men all over the country were being forced to go.

Clio suffered terribly when he went. We didn't hear from him for months. One day I was alone at my mother's apartment down the street from the dorm. Everyone always gathered at my mother's. My mother was as political as anyone. Clio and her boyfriend met there, side by side on the sofa that my mother had had in college. I was alone there one day, and the doorbell rang. I opened the door, and Clio's husband was standing there. His record had caught up with him and he'd been discharged. He was home.

Keith married the sister of the other leader of the student strike.

The personal and political lived deeply together in the 1960s. They intertwined and diverged, as the lives of the men and women of the 1960s intertwined and diverged, with and against politics. The ways we all had traveled were laid bare. Our lives were radical because the illusions covering them had been stripped away. And the violent cry that came from our war torn selves was "No More War."

We remember. Remembering is a funny state of mind. Sometimes it seems like trying to forget.

It is possible to relive what one once lived so intensely, in all its power and its bitterness. But it is also possible to see the past softened by time, and to love peace. In both are our salvation.

Like memory, art is about salvation. It is political in that it has a single feeling about life: that we were made for something better. It springs from love, and, like love, would have everything that is not love disappear from the world, and the world be wholly love.

With Kennedy's assassination in 1963 the country lost its illusions. The Reagan era attempted to piece them together. It did not succeed.

The antiwar movement was the war that cried "No More War." The personal is the political; the political is the personal. If we can remember truly, we can turn war each time to peace. Peace as real as war, as deep, as true, as profound. We can learn from what we did right. So help me God.

9. KEITH

When I met Keith, through a friend of mine at Radcliffe, in the fall of 1965, I was just emerging from my grief for Rick. I was a junior and Keith was an Advanced Placed freshman.

Keith was slight and acrobatic, with a habit of leaping into my arms when scared. He had fair hair and a Midwestern drawl. After I broke up with him, my mother told me, he started out at 1 a.m. for Northampton. The roads were snowy, he was ploughed, and he ran out of gas at about 2:30: no one in sight. He started to walk, and after a while he saw a light in the distance. He went on toward it, thinking all the while, "They'll be asleep, I'll have to wake them up; they'll be so cozy in bed and they'll hear a knock on the door, and me yelling, 'It's me! Open up! Gimme gas!' Oh, no," and he went on toward the light feeling guiltier and guiltier until when he got to the house he pounded madly on the door and when the farmer came down in his nightcap, Keith yelled, "You know what you can do with your goddamned gas!"

No, that's a story a friend told me, to illustrate a point.

The first Christmas Keith and I were together, we drove out to Akron, Ohio in a blizzard. We started off at 6 p.m. and by the time we reached Albany we couldn't see the road or any cars after a while. Keith hadn't slept in two weeks because of exams. We went over the center strip and swung back the other way. The car stopped in a drift. Keith was hallucinating bison. Somehow, I don't remember how, we got to a motel where we spent the night. I don't remember that, either. The next day the roads were ploughed and we sailed into Akron, which was covered with Christmas tree lights, right after dark.

Keith and I sort of decided to get married that week at his mother's house. His father had deserted the family the summer before, his best friend had gotten his girlfriend pregnant in Keith's house, and Keith had been thinking of becoming a priest till he met me. We spent the vacation playing sexual games, the kind three year olds play, and somehow when we stopped in New York on the way back Keith and I ended up in the diamond district with a diamond. He put it on my finger that evening before Jane's New Year's Eve party, saying, "Shine, Nan, shine tonight."

At Jane's I called Rick up and he came over with his fiancée. Jane tried to stop me, but I was determined. The rugs were rolled up in Jane's bedroom and there was a bright, empty space. That was the last time I saw Rick. He's dead now, and there's nothing to say about it except that I loved him more than I loved anyone else in the world.

It's funny. I've heard of a lot of college kids driving home on no sleep and hallucinating bison.

After I broke up with him, Keith drove down to Washington for an antiwar demonstration. When he came back he announced to my mother, "I have pissed on the Pentagon." He told her that all the marchers, when they wanted to take a leak, went up to the Pentagon wall, and he described relieving himself against it while a girl next to him took down her pants, and how they asked each other, "Where are you from?"

Anyway, what happened to Keith, he told my mother back then, was that he ran out of gas and ran into someone who said Keith could siphon out some of his gas, and in the process Keith swallowed about a teaspoonful of the stuff. He said thanks and drove off, and as he drove along he began to wonder what would happen to him now that he'd swallowed a teaspoonful of gas. So when he got to a roadside phone he looked up the local hospital in the directory and called them. "How much did you swallow?" the nurse on duty (it was now about 4 a.m.) asked him. "A teacupful?"

"Oh, no," Keith said, "about a teaspoonful." "Well, you should be all right," the nurse said, "but it's important not to vomit, because if you vomit, the gas could get into your lungs and cause a problem." Keith began wondering how he could be sure not to vomit, so he asked her. "Eat some charcoal, okay?" she said, and hung up.

Now Keith was lost on a lonely road without any charcoal, trying not to vomit. He lit a cigarette, and illumination struck. Larks had charcoal filters (to trap the gas) and his cigarettes were Larks! He peeled the paper off of his remaining cigarettes' filters, ate them, stretched out on the tops of the washers in a providential laundromat, and got a good morning's sleep.

When I broke up with Keith, right after my father got married, Keith came to me and said, "Do you know what's going on in your mother's apartment? Your sister is breaking up with *her* boyfriend." And that Thanksgiving, my mother said, planning the meal, "And when we all go up to the table to get our turkey and cranberry sauce, we'll say, 'Thank God I'm not engaged to Keith Atkins. Have a Lark.'" She also says, "Have a Lark" when I cry. I cried for four hours once, though (Rick, of course) and she didn't say a word. That was the best.

I have enough material to last a lifetime.

10. A QUESTION OF STYLE

My sister Mistletoe is a question of style.

I have a photograph of the two of us in the apple orchard in Vermont. We are wearing baggy sweaters and corduroy overalls. I am holding a large woven basket. I am about seven; Mistletoe is about four. I look remarkably serious. I have a high forehead and thick, dark hair. I am thinking, all the time.

Mistletoe has blond curls. She has one fist halfway to her mouth, and she is looking at the camera with a trusting, sunny expression that says, "Oh, really?"

With Mistletoe there is a question and there is a style.

I want to know and understand everything. Mistletoe says, quick, amused, interested, dubious, "Oh, really?" I had an answer. Mistletoe posed the question. Mistletoe stamped her foot, dressed in her petticoats, and demanded, "What about *my* say?"

This is slightly different from the half feelings, the little feelings, which Mistletoe suggests among the apple leaves.

Writing a story in a half voice is a way of saying, "It seems as though it should have been a big deal, but it wasn't important."

Mistletoe is relieved that certain of my stories are written in a half voice. But she says that people like the stories that they can understand. She isn't sure that people can understand those stories. She thinks that you have to write about states of mind from the outside.

I think that the way the facts were lived sometimes poses an embarrassing question, but determines the style of a story, a "true story." Maybe you cared and maybe you didn't. Maybe you were somewhere else at the time. In going back you might find what was hidden, or the hiddenness might be the point of the story. But you always go back to find out what to love and how to love.

Mistletoe was much too young for Elvis Presley when he became the top singer, and she thought that he was very funny. She took his song. "Love me tender, love me sweet," and sang,

> Love me tender, love me sweet,
> Love me like a pickled beet.
> Love me tender, love me true,
> Love me like an Irish stew.

She and Alma Tuchman, the historian Barbara Tuchman's daughter, who was in her class at Brearley, sang this to the telephone operator at the Tuchman's place in Cos Cob, and hung up. The operator called back and Mrs. Tuchman answered the phone. She said, "My daughter would never do such a thing. And by the way, while I have you on the phone, the telephone service is terrible down here."

Once in Vermont I was very seriously reading Dee Brown's *Bury My Heart at Wounded Knee*, which had just come out. Mistletoe looked at the cover and said, in great disdain, " 'Bury my heart at Wounded Knee?' Bury my knee at wounded *heart.*"

Mistletoe was sort of dour. She took the line from the song in the TV production of *Cinderella* which was supposed to be fantastically hopeful and when things got too much she would put her hand to her head and say, " 'Impossible things are happening every day!' " She also used to say when things got bad, quoting the love song, " 'Some things that happen for the first time seem to be happening again!' "

The stories are my father. My father laughed in wonder and love at life, *life,* when I got it right cried in joy and amazement, "*Ha!*" The book, the great continuum, the repository of all stories, is my mother. My mother is an enormous bee, humming in a great continuum. And the little feelings, like apple leaves, are my little sister.

Mistletoe and I stand side by side. Behind us are the apple trees. I say, courageously, "I can understand." Little Mistletoe, caught by surprise, one fist half way to her mouth, looks up, interested, skeptical, trusting, asking, "Oh, really?"

11. AT HOME ABROAD

In the summer of 1965 I went to Europe with Thalia. Thalia's family was Fifth Avenue New York, and they wouldn't let Thalia travel without a chaperone, so her grandmother Puddy led the entourage. We landed at Heathrow, then went from London to Ireland to Paris—half way down the Eiffel Tower the elevator got stuck, and as we hung over Paris for what seemed like an hour the elevator man looked down and said to Thalia, "Tie your shoe. You will fall."—to Rome to Venice, without, it became apparent, Thalia's having written to or called her parents. My mother says that the first letter she got from me was from the veined marble bathtub in our hotel suite in Rome. I had seen the translucent marble windows in the basilicas. The golden light made me want to sit down on the great floor like a child and stay forever. The conflicts which had been monumental at home were resolved all too easily abroad. These places were somewhere I could live. Rome was just like New York, with the same climate. I wrote my mother loving, beautiful letters describing what I saw. Padua, the Giottos, the mourning angels. Verona, the empty street, the balcony.

I was in the bathtub in the hotel suite in Venice when Puddy and Thalia began to fight about whether Thalia should call her parents. A vivid picture arose in my mind of Puddy's stepping into a gondola that morning. Puddy was stout, and wore flowing silken robes of lavender and gray, and turbans. She looked like something that should definitely stay on land. But Puddy contained an indomitable soul, equal to Thalia's, and if water was the way of travel, travel she would, and she sat in that gondola with all the grandeur of St. Mark's Dome, and looked as apposite. Puddy *was*, and that was enough. Thalia was in tears, and she was screaming, but she was losing the fight.

I was in no mood for fights. This was Europe, and I was euphoric. I didn't see how anyone could fight at a time like this. I decided to go to Switzerland, alone.

I took the train to Interlaken the next day. I had to change trains in Milan. I wanted to stay in Milan, to live there, to get an apartment. Milan had a golden, afternoon light. I felt completely at home.

On the train it was too dark to see the Alps. The man sitting opposite me asked if I was traveling alone. He said it was dangerous. "*Piccolo pericolo,*" I tossed off.

I had chosen Interlaken because my mother had gone there when she was young, and it had had a marvelous effect on her. A friend had once told my mother that she was "*dans la vrai.*" I thought that that was probably true, and I wanted to be there, too. My hotel room had one huge window that opened right on the Jungfrau. I lay in bed for ten days and looked at the Jung frau. It looked just like my mother. Then I took the train for Rome.

I'd wanted to stay in Interlaken in peace for the rest of my life, but the trip through the Alps in daylight was wilder than my wildest dreams. I felt as though I had been made for this. Europe was a mixture of sick peace and wild exhilaration. "So young," one of the clerks at the Interlaken hotel had said, "and so tired." I had worn a wide brimmed straw hat with ribbons and flowers the whole time, like a child. Now I felt like a radiant, beautiful woman, like Greta Garbo on a train, with that strange, inner peace amid chaos.

I met my friends with a great sense of culture shock, a mixture of guilt, relief, and horror. Our Alitalia flight was a day late getting into Rome. We slept in the airport. When we arrived in Athens, the boat that was to take us to the islands and to Istanbul had left. The boat line put us up in a hotel that was still under construction. There was hammering all night long. There was no heat. We all quarreled. We were completely undone. In the morning we took a taxi to the airport where a helicopter was to fly us to Crete to join our boat.

When the helicopter took off, I was terrified. I thought that it had all been a mistake. I knew I should have stayed in Interlaken. Under my feet was a *New York Times*. I picked it up to distract myself. It was dated the day before, Thursday, July 15, 1965. Across the front page the headline announced that Adlai Stevenson had died.

There I was in midair between Athens and Crete, and there was the *Times* bringing back to me everything I had ever known as home.

I had had a similar experience involving Stevenson when I was a child. We were in the house in Vermont, on the porch, at suppertime, my mother was eating corn on the cob, and, after a visit from her old philosophy professor, talking as she often did about the ultimate question being its own answer, and there was a conflict going on, and suddenly I found myself floating hundreds, thousands of miles above the earth. I could see the whole world, and I was looking down on people, people fighting. And I had thought that there must be a word, one word, which would solve the problem. I had wondered if Stevenson knew what it was. I was a good liberal child. I had thought that he might. Then I came down, and my mother was still eating corn on the cob.

That was how people felt about Stevenson. They thought that he knew the word.

And all of that seemed so long ago, in 1965, with Kennedy killed, and the war going on in Vietnam. It felt as though someone might have known the truth, once, and had never had the chance to say it, and everything after that had been a mistake. The way I'd felt that, if I stayed in Interlaken and looked at the Jungfrau long enough, I'd know the truth.

Chapter 11

In the clear waves of the Aegean were lines of blue black ink, like writing.

When we got back to Athens there were guns on the Acropolis—the colonels' coup. The city was closed to foreigners. Stay in your hotel or leave. We went to Delphi. The oracle was silent.

I spent the last month of the trip alone in Paris. Every night I ate *poulet basquaise* at a little restaurant by the Seine. Every conflict since the world began was resolved before my eyes every day in the Louvre and the Jeux de Paumes.

I was terrified to leave this precious Paris, and back in New York I walked up and down Broadway as if I were in a strange city, and ate dinner in unfamiliar restaurants, trying to be like my father, with whom I was staying, the man without a country. But when I got back to college, I knew the truth. The world existed. I'd seen it.

Eons later, in February, 1984, in Helsinki, I thought that the buildings looked very familiar. Some of them looked like Milan, and some of them looked like Leningrad. I mentioned this to a Finnish journalist who had fallen in love with me when I got acrophobia on the balcony of the National Museum in Stockholm. He was amazed. "Half of Helsinki was designed by the architect who designed Milan, and half was designed by the architect who designed Leningrad," he told me. I had never been to Leningrad, but I was also amazed. I really *had* seen Milan.

My father had told me to look up an old friend of his, a professor who had known my sister and me when we were children. When I phoned, he told me that he had been ill but that he was better now. I rang the bell and we sat in his beautiful Helsinki apartment with the golden Helsinki light, always afternoon in Helsinki in February. It was as though he had been waiting all those years for me to come. He told me how much we children had meant to him. He told me what it had been like to be with my father in New York, walking up and down Broadway all night while my father explained an idea he had just had, terrifically excited, swinging his arms. "I am not a genius," the man said. "I could never understand them. But to be there, to feel the excitement—it was truly exhilarating, wonderful. It was a privilege."

As he talked it came back to me as he had known it, truly, not in the cloudy way I'd known it as a child. He was telling me what the time of my parents' separation was really like. I had been waiting to hear what he had to say all my life. He had been waiting to tell me.

Several weeks after I got home, my father got a letter from the man's son. His father had died shortly after I left Helsinki. He had waited all that time, for me. And I had known that it was right to go to Helsinki in February.

12. HANOI

One evening in the Fall of 1966 a friend of Keith's from SDS came to me and asked me if I would go with a group of SDS students on a flight to Hanoi. Such flights were illegal then. He said that Keith couldn't go because he had an exam.

I went to the airport in a cotton skirt and sandals.

It was night. We were in the belly of a cargo plane. Wooden seats were arranged in a semicircle like those in auditorium.

Not many people had showed up.

People had brought guitars, and some people played. Eventually we just slept.

We woke up in Hanoi. Eager, grateful, welcoming hands reached out to us. We reached back, exhausted.

We were given fish and rice to eat.

There was a thunderstorm going on overhead. In the center of the town was a radio tower with loudspeakers. It was a U.S.-allied radio, and the voice was speaking in French, very loud. It said something about a curfew

Lightning hit the control tower and it collapsed.

As we stood there, an air raid siren started wailing. We saw some planes coming over the villages, dropping bombs. The bombs screamed as they fell. They exploded on the grass huts and on the earth, and dirt flew up in the air. We heard screams and we saw black, burned people, so burned we could only see the whites of their eyes, running out of the huts. Some of them took up sticks as makeshift crutches. It was Napalm that the planes were dropping, but I hadn't heard of it then. It set the people on fire—their hair stood straight up in flames, and their skin, which turn sort of reddish purple and black, peeled off. They were completely burned underneath, and insects started crawling over their bodies.

A river ran through the village, and it was red with blood. People ran to the river because they were burned. We saw naked children running down a road. A young woman who was working in a garden was burned and a firefighter hosed her off.

A plane came over the trees spreading defoliant behind it.

The aak-aak from the ground hit a plane. The tail burst into flames. It spiraled out of control and we could see people bailing out with parachutes. Sharp shooters hit them as they came down.

A lot of black smoke rose up from the fires on the ground. Firefighters with hoses were trying to put out the fires in the trees. The sun was covered by smoke.

Somehow I was holding a dead burned infant. I wouldn't believe that it was dead. They had to take it away from me. I was screaming. People had to hold me down.

I completely trusted these Vietnamese people.

The committee had sent us to an air raid shelter when the planes came overhead. It had white tile walls with green tile trim. Everyone was clinging to one another. Babies were screaming and their mothers were trying to shush and comfort them. Suddenly a bomb came right through the top of the air raid shelter. We had to evacuate the air raid shelter.

The air raid siren sounded the "all clear."

A man on the welcoming committee said, "This happens every day. All over the country."

The committee took us to a hotel. It was black with red lettering. We were fed large spicy shrimp with garlic and sesame, and, I think dog fish, and some kind of small baked turnovers. We also had something flat and hard, baked, like an unsweetened cookie, and pellets of bread.

Then they put us in a truck and took us to see a battlefield. Pure black and gray mud and one dead tree. They said that there was stagnant water standing in the field and that nothing would grow there, ever again.

They showed us a tiger cage.

They also showed us a coal mine, a copper mine, and a salt mine. At the coal mine there was a great pile of blueblack slag.

We walked through a field of grain.

The committee showed us a prison camp.

They took us to an airplane hanger. People in orange jumpsuits were working on the planes. Somehow I had gotten stuck in an elevator in the airport.

The head of the committee told us that they had malaria, chicken pox, whooping cough, and that they had no medicine or vaccines. He said that they were not able to operate on people who were crippled.

The committee was incredibly gracious and welcoming. They literally welcomed us with open arms. We said, "We are loyal American citizens and we are exercising our right to dissent."

We went to Haiphong Harbor. It was raining. A tiny boat was trying to make its way between huge waves created by the explosions of the mines that the Americans had put there.

They took us through one of the tunnels. We had to crawl on our bellies, pushing with our hands. It was a tight squeeze.

"We are not barbarians," one man told us. "We are a very ancient civilization."

Night had come. There was a red three-quarter moon.

Then we boarded the plane, hands waving behind us in farewell.

When I got back to the dorm, a friend said, "Where have you been? I've been looking for you all weekend."

"I was in Hanoi," I said.

"You went to Hanoi for the weekend?" she said incredulously. She usually went to New York.

We demonstrated at Dow Chemical, which made napalm, one of the main and worst weapons used against the Vietnamese. There were quite a lot of us. The police used tear gas. They grabbed me and tore a button off my blouse. We were all put in a police wagon. They took us to the courthouse. The judge took our names and released us.

I was afraid to read the papers during the Vietnam War. I was afraid I would read about Rick's death. I didn't watch the news. Instead, I wrote poetry, lots of it, to keep Rick alive. Rick was a writer and he thought I was a wonderful writer, and he was the inspiration for so much that I have done, both positive and negative. I identified with him so.

I worked for McCarthy and went to graduate school in English Literature at Boston College. I remember the Vietnam War, and more especially the assassinations of Martin Luther King, Jr. and Bobby Kennedy, as a dream of violence and mourning. My parents knew the left wing New York lawyer Leonard Boudin, and when the tragedy occurred at the Greenwich Village townhouse where his daughter Kathy Boudin, who belonged to the Weather Underground, an extremist antiwar organization, and other members, were making explosives that blew up and one of the members was killed, my mother was beside herself. "These times," she kept saying.

There is a French saying, "You only love one man all your life."

In my sophomore year at Radcliffe I walked into my mother's apartment and there was Rick. I thought I was going to faint. He was on his way to Maine. I thought that I would never see him again, and it was the most unbearable separation of my life.

I thought about him until I was thirty. I tried to call him every night for years at his apartment in New York, but the phone just rang and rang. Everything I did, writing, graduate school in English, even teaching, I did for him. He had gotten married and I didn't know where he was or how to get in touch with him.

When I was thirty, and teaching, I saw his sister's name in the Little Hollow newspaper. I wrote to her and asked her if she thought it would be all right if I got in touch with Rick, and where was he? I wanted to end the dream. I wanted whatever was reality. I was so afraid that he was dead.

His sister wrote back that she would ask her mother's opinion, and Rick's mother wrote to me that Rick was living in Reading, Pennsylvania, and doing very well. She gave me his P.O. box number.

I wrote to him. He wrote back, "I signed myself into a mental hospital when I heard from you. Don't write to me for six months." The next day I got a letter from him saying, "I signed myself out of the mental hospital. Let's get married. We'd have fantastic children."

This started the worst nightmare of my life, in which I tried to calm down Rick's conflicts about me, and couldn't. He wasn't "doing very well"; he was living in a Salvation Army mission. After about six months he killed himself. I don't know exactly what happened, but I had pleaded and pleaded with him to come and see me, always by letter, and in his last letter he wrote that he would. He said, " 'Barkus is willin.' " Twice he called me and I was out. If I could have talked to him—he didn't have a phone—I think that he might not have died.

This was the tragedy of my life, to have Rick dead, for so many years, and then, so briefly, alive again, and then dead.

After it happened I met Lionel Trilling's son, and I told him about it.

"That's the worst thing that could happen to anyone," he said.

When I was in graduate school and Terry had come back from studying with the pianist Nadia Boulanger in Paris, the brother of Terry's closest friend at Little Hollow was in the Weather Underground, and we used to hang out at their house on Franklin Street.

Chapter 12

Years later, my mother's friend Sylvia Wright and her husband bought the house and remodeled it.

Sylvia was a writer. In 1954 she published a piece in *Harper's Magazine* titled "The Death of Lady Mondegreen," in which she confessed to having heard, when she was a child, the Scottish ballad, "The Bonny Earl of Moray," as beginning

> Ye Highlands and ye Lowlands,
> O where hae ye been?
> They hae slain the Earl of Moray
> And Lady Mondegreen,

instead of

> And hae laid him on the green.

The piece consisted of other things she had misheard in childhood from poems, songs, sayings, the Bible, the Pledge of Allegiance: gladly the cross-eyed bear; God moves in mysterious ways; he wanders down a horn; Christ our royal master/Leans against the phone; one nation and a dirigible.

She coined the word "mondegreen." It exists in popular parlance, and the OED is working on it.

The piece ends, "Lady Mondegreen is me."

Sylvia was at the Radcliffe Institute working on a book about her aunt, Zina Faye, after whose family Faye House at Radcliffe is named. Zina was married to Charles Sanders Peirce. They had known Emerson and Hawthorne and the Alcotts. She wrote that Zina was her model. I had known Sylvia well since I was seven. She took me seriously, and it is because of her and of Jo March in *Little Women* that at seven I decided to be a writer.

Sylvia died of cancer in 1981. She wanted her memorial service to be a party for her friends. Harold Bloom read one of her poems. Ann Freedgood, who had been the editor-in-chief of Vintage Books at Random House and was a great friend of Sylvia and of my mother at Bryn Mawr and in New York, was there, and Pearl Kazin Bell. Pearl was a friend of Sylvia and my parents had known Alfred Kazin.

I met Harold Bloom once at Sylvia's in New Haven when she invited me down to hear Harold lecture on "Emerson and the Transparent Eyeball," and once later at Sylvia's memorial service. Sylvia had wanted it to be party for her friends. It was at Paul and Sylvia's house and all her friends were there, some in black, or gray, like me, but some in red. Nobody knew whether it was a party or a funeral. It was as if Sylvia had just stepped out to buy a quart of milk.

I was wearing the Greek belt buckle of Sylvia's that Paul had given me when I asked to have something of hers. Harold was there, and was to give a speech and read a poem of Sylvia's. I had been friends with Leslie and Susan Brisman at Vassar; Leslie was a protégée of Harold at Yale and I had also met him after Harold's lecture in New Haven. I wanted to talk to Harold. I introduced myself and we started talking about the Brisman's and their children. Harold said, "I'm going to get a drink. Don't go away." I stood there for a moment, alone and in agony, and then went to talk to a woman friend of Sylvia whom I had met before.

Then Harold was reading Sylvia's poem "Penelope" and weeping and talking a little. The poem was incredibly original.

I had last seen Sylvia on Patriot's Day of 1978, just before she died. She had been in great pain from the cancer and her doctor had given her morphine. It had made her delirious and Paul told me that she had been up all night screaming, "I'm going to die!" It was the morning after that morning that I went to their house on Franklin Street. Sylvia was sitting up in bed with practically no hair and Paul was sitting in an armchair at her bedside which I think he rarely left. They were watching the Marathon on TV. Everyone was very tense but very cheerful and calm.

Sylvia had been trying to finish her book, "Zina." She had been typing and typing. She died before she had written the final chapter.

Chapter 12

I had been wanting to talk to Harold ever since that last broken off conversation, so when I was trying once again to get "Zina" published I called him up. It was as though we had always been talking and we had never stopped. He said that a day didn't go by when he and his wife didn't think of Sylvia, that there had never been any one like her. It's true.

13. AN ELECTRON

My grandmother was a Force, my mother is an Element. My favorite course at college was called "The Enterprise of Science." When I read in Whitehead, whose house was around the corner from ours, the sentence, "An electron is its whole field of force," I went *bam*. I knew what I was.

My mother and Mistletoe had moved with me from New York when I came to college, and were living in a tiny apartment in Cambridge just down the street from me. Sometimes we tried to pretend that the others didn't exist. Sometimes we collapsed in a heap like the heaps of stuff in the apartment. Nothing was to be missing. If the bird won't stay in the nest, the nest will come back to the bird.

Mistletoe had wanted to be a ballerina in the apartment in New York where she was bored, and she used to swirl around the living room in all her petticoats, trying to do what nobody else was doing, that is, something. She did something. She made me want to marry her. In our new place in Cambridge, when she was twenty-three, she announced that she was getting married to Harvey. I got hysterical. I cried. I said, "You can't do this to me. *I* want to marry you!" Mistletoe sat on the edge of the bed in the room that had been hers all though high school, and had been left over when she came to college, and rubbed my back. "It has to be," she said. Now every night, when I'm hysterical over my love for Rick and his suicide, and what I've lost, I imagine that someone like Mistletoe, who has moved to Seattle with Harvey, is rubbing my back. I remember her crying, screaming on that bed, so that the boy next door could hear how *furious* she was that he didn't love her.

At Mistletoe's wedding we waited a long time on the lawn by the lake, and almost as an afterthought Harvey appeared, leading Mistletoe by the hand. The words were slowly spoken and then the song was over. And for a moment I thought I would burst, explode into a thousand pieces, all my energy leashed on the world. Then I saw the group that was quietly standing around me, covering me.

Mistletoe had walked to Buckingham and back every day with my mother's friend Annette's daughter. Annette and her daughter were both extremely beautiful, each in her own way. One day Annette was working in her tiny garden and her leg gave way and she fell on the flagstones. Her doctor found a brain tumor.

My mother went to the see her in the hospital every day. All of Annette's other friends deserted her. Her relatives came to divide up her jewels. It was a terrible hospital, and a long drive, but my mother went every day. When she left, Annette always asked, "Will you come tomorrow?" One day my mother asked Annette, "What does it mean to you that I come every day?" Annette said, "That you're *there*."

One day my mother came into Annette's room and Annette was sitting bolt upright in bed. "Hi, Annette," said my mother. "A is for paranoia," Annette said. "No, Annette," said my mother, "A is for Annette." Annette burst into tears, and everything was all right. The doctors were terrible. One doctor told my mother, "We can't deal with death."

One day my mother came and Annette was dying. My mother got into bed with her and held her until she had died. She came home and told us just that. But she remained the repository of all stories.

Several years later, when I had graduated and was teaching and home for vacation, it was my birthday, and we had a party. In the middle of it, the phone rang. It was Julie, who had once lived across the street, saying that she was at Newton-Wellesley Hospital with her husband. He'd had a bad heart attack. Julie was hysterical.

My mother called a taxi and went. The party broke up, and so did my nerves, and I sat alone and cried for three hours in outrage at life until my mother reappeared with the taxi driver who came in and had a drink with us. I couldn't stop crying. It was as though all the pain and rage I'd ever felt came pouring out. My mother said to the taxi driver, "I couldn't have managed without you," and he left. I went on crying. My mother sat there in a chair, still holding her purse on her lap, gazing in the distance with a look of pure disgust on her face. Julie's husband had died. Julie had never been happy until she met him. It was brief. My mother stared straight ahead for a long time, and the look on her face summed up everything one feels about "reality." "You're lucky you can cry like that," she said.

My grandmother was a Force. The day she died I was out painting the crabapple tree in the yard next door. I heard the phone and came in. It was a beautiful day. For three days after, everything around me looked like my grandmother. The secretary desk, the house across the street. I saw her everywhere. On the fourth morning I got up and looked out, and I saw her presence rising with the mist from the world, dispersed among the elements. Objects resumed their normal aspects.

"She never left," I said to my mother. "*Why?*" she asked. "She was a Force," I told her.

14. DEBRIS

My mother is an Element. Earth, air, fire, water. She also turned out to be the kind of element that has a half-life. She told me proudly that my cousin's friend Bert, who was into astrology, announced that she was "a very old life." There was a lot of debris.

She left some of it in Shepard Street when, at the change of the moon or the end of a half-life, she moved West to Seattle to be with Mistletoe and her children. The debris sat in piles, colorless, odorless, tasteless, sympathetic and sentimental. She shed her skin. From the West came motions of Earth, Air, Fire, Water.

The question was what to do with all that was left behind. She existed here in a missing state. The characteristic of the debris was to say, I'm missing.

I was housecleaning. The scraps and threads and strips of rag that composed this nest I had woven for myself, and which was woven for me, had disappeared. Form had taken their place. Dark, hot, elemental form. Anyone would have known that who looked at the place then. There was no more "I'm missing." There was only what was there.

Could what was there come back? It had always been there, just as my elemental mother was forever missing. Those touching piles of sweaters, those socks. Those sweaters that still were filled with her bosom. That bosom which contained all the elements.

The elements in the story flew back like string in the beaks of birds returning in the Spring. Only the nest had changed. It wasn't a covering over. It was hot, dark pocket where hearts beat and hunger piped. And the music, the sound of the thrush in Spring, said, "I am here, there, and everywhere." Music like water stuffed full of human emotion. My mother was human emotion. She was the stuff of life. The stuff of dreams. There was a lot of stuff going on in the apartment.

Yeasty stuff, and when it subsided, there were fragile arteries to be cleared of age-old blockages. That was the joy.

My grandparents had a great many objects, and these were divided up and portioned out before they died. My mother mentioned a relative who had been in Lincoln's cabinet. "Who got Lincoln's cabinet?" I asked. When they died, there was stuff remaining. It arrived in loads. "Somebody must have died," I thought. But they had already died. I thought, "The stuff died."

But it doesn't, you know. It's the mail that sits on everything like snow, like sea gull droppings. It's the present, the day to day, which immerses the earth in finitude, in pathos. The real stuff, the past, doesn't die. It comes alive in order to—in order to straighten one out. That carved chair, the glass-paned secretary with its grotesque dark wood. What more is wanting?

What is missing?

I wrote my mother a song:

> I'll be in Seattle when the rain falls
> you can count on it, I'll be there
> I'll see you in September
> by Puget Sound;
> when the drops start falling,
> I'll be around
> winter in Seattle
> is damp and gray
> I wouldn't miss it –
> oh, that snow, kiss it goodbye!
> the drizzle will be starting
> any day
> I can't wait
> just catch a freight

and be warm in the Lake Union Mist
instead of being cold and pissed

Deception Pass, I'm coming!
I see you in my dreams
when the showers start,
you'll hear "toot toot!"
and I'll get off the train
with a bumbershoot –
those sweet, wet
days, oh my!

15. WHY I LOVE MISTLETOE

Mistletoe's first day at Radcliffe, in September of 1966, was different from mine. I had Thalia with her chauffeur and her white gloves asking, "What's prince?" when everyone was fixing up her room and said, "Now let's go to Harvard Square and get prints." Mistletoe told me once, when I was complaining of men trouble, that when she first walked into her dorm, a girl who she later found out was named Elvira Oliver was sitting in a chair in the living room moaning, "Oh, I wish Gordon Linen would get here. I can't wait for Gordon Linen." Mistletoe thought that Gordon Linen must be some fantastic boy. It turned out to be the linen service.

Mistletoe's friends were more practical than mine, and more mysterious. Mistletoe loves all kinds of women of different shapes and sizes, attitudes and quirks. She loves fat women and skinny women, pregnant women and grandmothers. When Lydia Davis, whom I had been at boarding school with and who is now a well-known writer, came down to stay with my sister and my mother for a weekend when Mistletoe was still in high school, Mistletoe thought she was wonderful because when she and Mistletoe sat on the sofa and talked for two hours, the girl ate a whole loaf of Portuguese sweet bread. Mistletoe thought that that was great. She was lucky enough to have as a roommate at Radcliffe Judy Norsigian, one of the founders of the *Our Bodies/Ourselves* collective.

Because the historian Barbara Tuchman's daughter Alma was in my sister's class at Brearley, we knew Mrs. Tuchman quite well.

Chapter 15

She was wonderful. One day my mother went over to Barbara Tuchman's apartment on some school business. Mrs. Tuchman was alone, and afterwards, when my mother was going down in the elevator, a man told her that Barbara Tuchman had won the Pulitzer Prize that morning. When my mother got home she called up Mrs. Tuchman and asked her if she would like to come over for a drink, but Mrs. Tuchman said she thought she'd better stay home to answer the phone calls.

Barbara Tuchman gave my Commencement address at Radcliffe. Her daughter Jessica was in my class. She said, "Girls, how can you complain about the rooms at Radcliffe and sleeping in bunk beds when you're getting such a terrific education?" And then she turned around and endowed Tuchman Hall, the snazziest dorm at Radcliffe. I used to imitate her: "Girls, how can you complain about sleeping in bunk beds? Henry Ford said, '*History* is bunk.'" She made bunks history.

In high school Mistletoe had baby sat for the family down the street from us. She thought that the woman was perfect. "Everyone should be like Persephone," she told me seriously. Persephone went to a party two hours late because she couldn't find a stocking without a run in it. She finally went with a run in her stocking. Mistletoe told me other things that Persephone had done, building up her case. She liked people who didn't care what other people thought of them. I thought that Mistletoe was the sweetest, funniest, subtlest thing I'd ever seen. And she got all the highest possible scores on her College Boards, which is more than I did.

When Mistletoe was getting married, after Radcliffe, she wanted to invite her high school math teacher and English teacher and the Headmistress. I couldn't imagine doing such a thing. To me it would have been a regression. But later I gave in. I told Mistletoe that I thought that I would write to the woman who was Head of the Middle School at our girls' school in New York and ask her what had happened to me. Mistletoe said lovingly that she thought that this was a very good idea.

I said to Mistletoe recently that I had trouble telling people apart. "I mean," I said, "What's the difference between Stevie and Einstein?" Stevie was the woman who taught carpentry at the girl's school, and she was the most wonderful person in the world. "No difference at all," said Mistletoe lovingly. Mistletoe is very sensible.

She had been beautiful when I came home on Thanksgiving from Little Hollow. She and my mother met me at Grand Central, and Mistletoe was wearing a red sleeveless knit suit—and she was thin, and she had a figure. And one day I walked into our bedroom and she was trying on a pale blue Japanese silk dress—what they used to call a "sheath"—in front of the mirror, and it fitted her to perfection. I nearly cried. In my brief absence she had blossomed. She was no longer Miss L. Toe who wanted to be a ballerina and danced around the living room in all her petticoats. She was something new.

All the boys who came down with me from Little Hollow loved her, and some wanted her. Rick adored her. One day she came into the living room in a straight blue cotton shirtdress. Rick looked up and said, "It would look great dripping wet." He was one of the most open, loving people I've ever known.

In Randolph we used to drive by an old house with a hand lettered sign outside saying "Night crawlers." Mistletoe stood it as long as she could, and then one day as we drove by it she asked, "Nana, *what* are night crawlers?"

The bakery downtown had delicious crullers, and my friend Bonnie Hiller said when I told her that my mother had died, "She was like a mother to me," and she remembered eating night crullers on the beds on the porch.

I never have words to describe people with, so much so that when I start to describe someone to a friend, he or she always says, "Never mind. I'll have to meet them." But I know that Mistletoe is subtle, because the poet we called The Poet who lived on the second hill over when we were children in the summers in Vermont—the one who, when he'd talked all afternoon and finally his wife insisted that they leave as it was way past dinner time and everyone was starving, and he couldn't think of an exit line, exclaimed, "The world is full of bastards and bitches, / And so say I in my corduroy breeches"—The Poet said to me after meeting us a couple of times, "Your sister is subtle and you're profound." That's why I love Mistletoe.

16. "MISS AMERICAN PIE"

In 1973 I received my Ph.D. in English Literature and got a job teaching at a small, prestigious liberal arts college.

My great aunts had gone there, and one of them, Mary Jordan, had been a professor at Smith College. She was one of the first women academics. One of my aunts had taught there, and two of them had gone there. My great uncle had given all the bathrooms in the main building.

The campus looked like Paradise. I walked home from teaching past honeysuckle and violets.

It was like Vermont, and Chapel Hill, and of course in many ways like home.

My apartment was the wing of a building on the outskirts of the campus.

I had been politically active, but it really wasn't until I was teaching that I became radicalized. Before, I had been a student, but now I had responsibility for students, and I found myself in the position of trying to protect them from some of the more senior figures in the college.

The year before I came there had been a great deal of unrest among the Black students. They had made demands and taken actions, but nothing had been resolved. The cloud of these stories hung over the start of my teaching.

At nine o'clock on the first morning of classes I walked into my Freshman English section and saw that the class was about equally divided, Black and white, with a large number of empty seats in between. I had been hired in June, I was a "to be announced" in the catalogue, and it turned out that all the Black Freshman English students had been segregated into my section.

The Black Students would not read *Dubliners*, so we compromised on an anthology of Black poetry, *Black Voices*, and *Dubliners*. The atmosphere warmed up for a while, but soon I could see that all was not well. When I asked the students why, the Black students told me that the scholarships, mandated by HEW, of those who had been recruited, some from the South and some from Harlem, were being cut back, and that they would have to leave.

This was completely illegal. I went to my chairman, thinking that there was some mistake.

"I'm sure you're doing a great job," he said. "I hate freshmen. I hate Blacks. Keep it out of my office, okay?"

I went to the Dean, who was Acting President.

"What a shocking way to run a college," she said, running the college. "Now, I'm very busy. Good day."

I got up to leave.

She said, "Oh, one more thing. Do you go to faculty tea?"

I said, "No."

"You should go," she said. "You might like to meet our" she held up one finger "Black faculty member."

The recruited Black students' scholarships were rescinded, and they left.

I had grown up in Chapel Hill and had very strong, warm feelings for Blacks. They felt familiar to me, like home.

I remained close to some of the others as a teacher for as long as I stayed.

The next year there was a movement on the part of the administration and trustees to cut faculty salaries. A questionnaire was sent to all students, asking whether they would rather have their tuition raised or faculty salaries cut. The students didn't really know what was going on, and of course they answered, the latter.

The faculty wanted to have a work slow down, more directed at the students than at the administration. Everything was in confusion. Teaching came to a virtual standstill.

The students still didn't know what was going on, and they were miserable. I explained the situation to them.

There was to be a faculty meeting on the subject of cutting faculty salaries the next day. My students asked if they could come to it. I said yes.

I had had enough bad experiences with teachers and administrators at Harvard to put me on the students' side every time. I was popular with the students, and I took what I felt to be my responsibilities toward them seriously enough to take certain risks.

A number of students came into the faculty meeting with me. It was against college policy to allow students in a faculty meeting. A whisper went up around the room. "*Students! Students!*" Students were the adversary at the moment.

I stood up and made a speech.

After the meeting, a woman economist came up to me and said, "*I* know who you are! I've seen you around, but I didn't recognize you. You're Herbert Robbins's daughter!"

"I remember you now," I said. "It was a long time ago. You had an apartment in the Village, with a clavichord. It's funny, but I've always imagined the first meetings of the women's movement taking place in that apartment."

"When I heard you doing your impassioned thing," she said, "I thought, 'My God, that's Herbert Robbins' daughter.'"

I spent the summer of Watergate, the debacle which brought down the Nixon presidency, lying on the floor of my Cambridge apartment on Linnaean Street, which I kept while I was teaching, in front of the fan—it was very hot—watching the Watergate hearings on television and talking to my mother, who was watching it in her Shepard Street apartment, on the phone. It was great. She liked Woodward and Bernstein, the reporters who had broken the story for *The Washington Post*, and Sam Dash, the prosecutor. I liked Sam Ervin, the head of the congressional committee holding the hearings, and Inouye, the Senator, from Hawaii, and Tony Ulasewicz, a terribly funny Washington cabdriver who was a witness.

There was a program recently on public television about Watergate thirty years after. At the end someone said that the lesson of Watergate hadn't been learned: that the president is not above the law. I'm afraid that that is exactly what we are seeing now.

Judith Wax wrote a wonderful poem after Chaucer about Watergate, "The Waterbury Tales," which appeared in the *New Yorker*. It told of all the characters in the Watergate story: "An Ehrlichman there was . . . ," "A Haldeman there was . . . ." I routinely taught a course called "Chaucer to Pope," the Shakespeare course, intermediate writing courses, and Freshman English. In the fall I started "Chaucer to Pope" off with "The Waterbury Tales."

At the end of my father's life we were talking about it. "Whatever happened to Judith Wax?" he said.

Eventually I resigned from the college. All the younger Jewish members of my department were losing their jobs. Out of 217 faculty members, only 14 were Jewish. I am half Jewish, on my father's side, and while I think no one knew *what* I was and was dying to find out, my chances at tenure looked good.

I left in 1976. The Vietnam War was over, and I came home.

Rick died shortly after I left, after six months of correspondence in which he talked alternately of marrying me and of killing himself. I do not know exactly what happened, but I know that he called the rabbi who was the only person he knew in Reading and asked him to drive him to the hospital. He told him he had had a fight about drugs, and he was hallucinating. The hospital gave him a shot of Prolixin, which he had told me he got every month and which made him unable to see or walk or read for two weeks each time, and let him go. It seems that he jumped off a viaduct over a tennis court which John Updike had written about, in Reading, Pennsylvania, and which Rick had often talked and written about jumping off of.

I know that at the funeral the rabbi said, "Rick was a good person."

He was.

When John Berryman jumped off a bridge I instantly knew how Rick would do it, and that it would not be over water but over pavement. That was when I was in graduate school, and had not been in touch with him for many years. When I did write to him, I knew immediately from his first letter what would happen. The next six months were a nightmare in which I tried to prevent what I had foreseen, and could not.

After Christmas I got a telegram from his mother.

I was alone. I put Mozart's 22nd Piano Concerto on the record player.

For a moment I thought I would go out of my mind with loss.

Then I heard a voice, a man's voice, very loud and definite, saying, "A different fate is reserved for you. You will go on to suffer and create."

17. A MATTER OF TASTE

Crystal Christiansen, in her silver sheath, swarmed into the cubicle where I was lying, wrapped in gravesheets, on the examining table. "This is my assistant, Dr. Kent," she pointed at a man and a woman two steps behind her. "She's had an operation for endometriosis," she explained over her shoulder to Dr. Kent as she parted the lips of my vagina and inserted her cold fingers. "The possibility that she has another cyst should not be dismissed. I don't feel anything," she said, still over her shoulder. Then, turning her head away altogether, "Was it a chocolate cyst?" "No, I don't think so," I said. Then I said, "What's a chocolate cyst?" "One filled with blood," she removed her red lacquered fingernails. "You can get dressed now."

"Did you like Crystal Christiansen?" a friend asked me. Her little worn face always looked as though it were raised to be kissed. "Yah," I said, "I liked her a lot. I trusted her because I thought she was so busy being Crystal Christiansen that she'd leave you alone." "Well," she said, and her mouth puckered a little oddly, "it's a matter of taste."

The other day someone asked me why I liked Nick, and I said, "Because he's familiar." But I might have said, "It's a matter of taste." I mean, he's just like my father. When I was hardly more than a child, and in love with Rick, and deserted by him, I lay on the living room floor and dreamed of writing a book called *The*

Philosopher's Wife, or, Taste. But that didn't work; Rick tasted terrible, like burnt rubber.

I loved Nick with the same love with which I loved Rick, which is, and which makes things, impossible.

Somewhere a psychologist describes the way a baby feels when it puts food in its mouth for the first time, the expression on its face. "Hmm, what *is* this? What's *happening* to me? Do I *like* it?" Taste. Ambiguity. Chacun a son goo.

It's a clear case of ambiguity. Nick came over at midnight one night, and suddenly, after a few more beers, he felt enormously sick and he couldn't get it out. He sat there heaving with anxiety while I rubbed his back and whispered, "It's all right, relax, I love you, I think you're wonderful, you have no idea what you mean to me," and he sweated and shook and put his head in his hands and said, "I'm sorry, I'm sorry, I shouldn't be here, I should be alone." It was exactly like Rick, except that since Rick's death I've become permanently drained and I couldn't feel much except how exactly like Rick it *was*. Nick was so afraid to puke, and he wanted to so much, and he lay on the sofa until I said, "I just wish you'd puke and get it over with," and made him drink some bicarbonate of soda, telling him my grandmother always said, "You never know *what* will happen when you take soda," and when he came out of the bathroom radiant, he said, "It's a boy."

And a couple of months later, after we had made love tentatively for the first time in a long time and were alone together the next time, we wore down each other's wills with restraint until suddenly I was hysterical and I swam over to him saying what the therapist had said that we had been laughing at in the book I had been reading, when she called someone, crying, at 3 a.m.: "I have be to irrational," and I was.

The relationship is a place to get all the *trying* out; Nick trying for taste so hard, sitting bent over with agony, doesn't *anyone* have taste—and I say, relax, it's all right; I'm here, you're a spoiled child who wants nothing but taste—nothing but the best taste will do—you want a star, up in the sky—a star that you can put in your pocket with your appointment book—a star for trying so hard—*don't try so hard*, you're killing me—

Nick interviewing away, day after day, without a break—a reporter—well, how vicarious *can* you get? Let's find out—leaving at 3 a.m. because the heart transplant might call him at any time—asking probing questions—well, I said, that's quite a responsibility—and whose heart is it, anyway? god knows I love you, but that's not it.

did anyone ever exist who was really like this?

it's not the end of the world.

Nick's father died of Alzheimer's several years later. When he was very sick Nick used to come and sit on the sofa and cry and cry.

He appeared at the door one morning. "My father died," he said. He had been up with him all night in the nursing home. He was delirious with exhaustion and grief. His family was Catholic and the open casket funeral was to be on Sunday, "I have to get a haircut," he kept saying.

He told me that the funeral seemed surreal. "I had to stand in a reception line and shake hands with hundreds of people I'd never met, and my father was lying right there."

On the first anniversary of his father's death, I was awakened from a dream of a wild police chase by the telephone at 3 a.m. It was Nick. He'd been arrested driving ninety miles an hour on the wrong side of the road. He didn't remember anything about it. He was in jail.

A friend bailed him out and at 5 a.m. I called a friend of mine whose husband was a lawyer. My mother wrote a letter to the judge as the daughter of another well-known judge and Nick got probation.

Once Nick flew to upstate New York to see a brother to whom he was not very close. He was nervous about it. The day after he left I felt extremely sick and had to go to bed. I wondered why. I wasn't dependent on Nick in that way.

I fell asleep and dreamed that I was staggering up the red carpet covered steps in the foyer of the Georges Cinque in Paris naked and clinging to the brass railing.

Nick called me the next day. "I'm back," he said.

"Why did you come back so soon?" I asked. "I thought you were going to stay for a week."

"I was," Nick said, "but last night my brother and I sat up very late talking about my family and drinking beer and I got very upset. I went down to sleep in the spare room in the basement and when I woke up I felt so sick I couldn't move. I finally hauled myself up the stairs by holding onto the banister, completely naked, and when I got upstairs I have never been so sick in my life. So I got a ticket and came home."

When Nick was on probation I wrote him a letter. I wrote, "One of my boyfriends is dead and another is on probation and it's not making me happy at all. If you won't do it for your own sake, do it for my sake, but stop drinking."

Nick never said anything to me about the letter, but he told a mutual friend that it was the best thing anyone had ever done for him, and he stopped drinking.

18. YOU'LL NEVER BE THE SAME

Actually, after Nick left, everything came together and I burst out with a musical. The libretto follows. It's called

YOU'LL NEVER BE THE SAME

ACT I
(Noni's father appears in spot light, stage left)

Noni's father (song):
        when the world is topsy-turvy,
        women skinny or men curvy,
        and you want to take a little break,
        then you curl up by the fire,
        and you hope it will inspire
        great thoughts in the break you take,
        but you'll find your apparatus on the blink:
        no, you don't know what to think.

        some people don't know what
        to say, or in a rut,
        they don't know what to do, but
        your problem is more real,
        even, than not knowing what to feel.

        some take a lot of trouble

Chapter 18

        to execute a double
        play upon the baseball field;
        some people want to gamble,
        and some would rather ramble,
        and some find Joseph Campbell
        gives a significant yield,
        but if your wants are modest,
        you'll find it is the oddest
        thing you can imagine (need a drink?)
        when you don't know what to think.

        chorus: (song)
        oh, show me
        the way to the libido,
        show me
        the way to go home.
        you can take a vaporetto to the Lido,
        you can fly Air Alaska to Nome,
        you can drive a car
        out to the sticks
        or ride a pony
        if you're hicks,
        but show me
        the way to the libido:
        is it a painting, or a poem?
        show me
        the way to the libido
        pleasure dome.

Noni (song):

        I'm a slow waker upper.
        Took me a long time to wake up to the fact
        that I'm a slow waker upper,
        takes me a long time to be able to act
        in the morning, the morning,
        oh, then I'm all thumbs,
        can't wait till the evening,
        the evening comes,

'cause then I'm with my baby,
and I'll tell you certain sure
that then there's no maybe
about what I'm doing or what I'm doing it for.

But baby, if you have to tell me
something I gotta know,
whatever you're going to sell me,
sell it to me slow

'cause I'm a slow waker upper,
and when I wake up from this dream,
I'll tell you, baby,
that I'm going to scream
'cause I'm a slow waker upper, etc.

ACT II
Scene: Nick and Noni
Noni (song):
    I'm either high, or I'm depressed,
    there's nothing in between.
    I don't know beans about the rest,
    the golden "fine, thanks," mean.
    terrible and great are my emotions,
    they flow in me like tides within the oceans.
    and, dear, it's wonderful to love you so,
    and awful, too:
    I'm fabulous
    because I'm blue.

(Nick moves closer) Nick (song):
    you've either got it
    or you don't:
    it's not for me to say
    if you will use it
    or you won't
    and throw it all away,

gut level feelings
of originality
pass like bad dealings
between you and me.
you either know
or you don't know:
I can't tell you,
you see,
but baby, if I love you so
it's sure that you love me.

Nick and Noni (song):

I'm in an impossible situation,
I'll leave nothing to your imagination:
I'm other-directed
and there's nobody other than you:
boop a doo doo

if you're inner directed
you can tighten your belt
if there's nobody else in view,
if you're outer-directed
you can get your kicks
from licking the problems
that everyone licks
but I'm other directed
and there's nobody other than you:
boop a doo doo.

Noni (song):

it's funny to know,
I usually just guess,
usually go
with the guys who are just so-so,
so, so so-so,
so that a yes
is no more false than true,
but, baby, I know,
know that it's you.

You'll Never Be the Same

    it's funny to feel,
    feel I know what I'm doing,
    feel that it's real,
    by God, and worth pursuing,
    so I pursue you,
    and, oh, the time I spend ruing
    every old shady deal.

Nick and Noni (song):
    who's to know
    whether we're right or wrong,
    who's to tell us
    what we've known all along,
    who's to say
    if what we feel is true:
    nobody
    but me and you.
    who's to know
    whether we waste our time,
    who's to know,
    who's to know.
(they go to the bed and lie down) (darkness)

(lights come up, Noni rises, stretches)
Noni (song):
    a heterosexual love
    is what you are to me:
    two bodies, different in kind
    as they can be
    if you're my father
    and I'm your mother
    then weren't we made
    for one another?

    a heterosexual love
    is what you are to me,
    the basic similarity
    is all in mind:

            our bodies
            are totally distinct in kind.
(Nick gets up, they end hand in hand)

ACT III
Scene: classroom with students, mixed genders
Students (with rock band) (song):
            when depression hits,
            the banks are closed,
            supplies cut off,
            are you supposed
            to put up with this?
            no, no, no,
            grab your hat,
            shut the door and go:
            beg, borrow or steal
            love today.

            when the state is in
            an awful state,
            no one knows
            what's love, what's hate
            bands of marauders
            rule the scene,
            hard to tell
            just what things mean:
            beg, borrow or steal
            love today.

Students (song):
            please excuse, Doctor Marcuse,
            we're trying to find a way,
            nothing fancy, obscure or chancy,
            of getting through the day.

            if life's treasure

You'll Never Be the Same

        is love's sweet pleasure
        please make the way clear.
        give us a system,
        and we'll resist 'em:
        we swear to hold it dear.

        please excuse, Herbert Marcuse,
        if we're funereal:
        we're caught between
        the obscene
        and the ethereal.

(Nixon has been glowering in the corner. Now spot light on him, stage left)
Nixon (song):

        I wonder who's Kissinger now,
        I wonder who's teaching Bill how
        I wonder if he
        talks of '73:
        I wonder who's Kissinger now

        I wonder who's ruling the state,
        or if that idea's out of date,
        and whether, at last,
        I'm a thing of the past:
        I wonder who's Kissinger now.

(Noni rises from amid the students: spot light)
Noni (song):

        Oh, it would be delish
        if I could have one wish:
        I wish the state would wither away.
        and though you may say, pish,
        I wouldn't give a knish
        for proof it might not happen today.

        everybody happy, and thanking their luck,
        there won't be anywhere to pass the buck:
        the state will collapse like an old dinosaur,

for that's what states are for.

now, I don't mean to sound sad or make a fuss,
but right now, it seems, the state is withering us,
and if we don't cooperate
    and expand the personal sphere,
the state will with us away, I fear.
but perhaps it will give one last tax hike and collapse,
perhaps, perhaps, perhaps, perhaps,
give one convulsive pressure and breathe its last,
for we're already living in the past.
oh, the state has a monopoly on me:
sing hey, for blissful anarchy.

so everybody dance and paint their song:
how long, oh lord, how long?

EPILOGUE

Noni (song):

I'm getting sick of being
absolutely marvelous,
a miracle worth seeing,
who never makes a fuss.
I'm getting tired of always
being at my best,
no matter what any asshole says,
or who's a goddamn pest.
what life has taught me
isn't always clear:
don't repress, suppress –
is that it, dear?
but I'm a bit bored
with the present mode
and I think that I can afford
to explode!

(loud musical pastiche of all the songs, all characters singing, dancing, cartwheels, etc.) FINIS

Herbert Marcuse was a radical who taught at Brandeis and was very well known in the 1960s. Henry Kissinger was Richard Nixon's Secretary of State.

19. FISH

```
                b
            a a r
            f d e y
          a t   a o
          b l e f l u d f
        y e l r i l   e r s
        o e     s y s a i i d
    i u n n e h   e d e s a o n
  f v   i a   c e   n t n r o
    e u g t y a   b d e c   t
      p h i o r y o s r e
        t n u e o y
          g     u
            d i r
            o f
            n
            t
```

20. WHAT IT ISN'T

Coming out of male-dominated, competitive academia into the woman's movement in the mid-1970s was heaven. I began to identify myself as a woman, which meant not only editing but painting, like my mother and like my father's sister Francie Shumsky, who was a painter and a sculptor. Her husband Sherman and his brothers owned Shumsky's restaurant in Atlantic City, where all the convention people used to congregate in the evening. Sherman met a lot of well-known people, including journalists, and brought them home.

One day I woke up from a nap and I had to get to the bank by three o'clock. I ran out without drinking any tea or coffee or even having a cigarette. All the way to Harvard Square, and at Holyoke Center, I saw visions of people in their natural glory—working people, secretaries, street people—like Blake's "the human form divine."

When I was studying art in Cambridge I took singing lessons from an old Dutch woman, Tina Rolf, whom I met in my neighborhood. She was a wonderful teacher. She and her husband had spent a great deal of time in Africa, and their two-story condominium was filled with African fabrics, on the couches, the cushions, the walls. I studied with her for a year, and then she said, "You have a good voice, and you have a *lot* of voice, but I don't know what to *do* with you." So I took my guitar and went to Harvard Square and sang.

In 1986 I published my collection of poems and etchings, *Amelie*, with Effie Mihopoulos at Ommation Press. It was a political women's movement statement. I was standing outside a display of the book in the window of the Cambridge Trust in Harvard Square when Professor John Finley came along. He had recently lost his wife. I said hello to him, and I said, "This is my book." He looked at it, and then he asked, "Are you married?" I said no. "Married to your imagination," he said, and walked on.

Lawrence Ferlinghetti was supposed to give a reading at the Old Cambridge Baptist Church in Cambridge. I went, but there was a sign on the door saying that the reading was postponed. I couldn't go at the new time. I called Ferlinghetti, who had been a great hero of mine ever since I had read *A Coney Island of the Mind* when I was at Little Hollow. He was extremely nice, and I have some letters from him about my work.

My neighbors at that time included David Riesman, the author of *The Lonely Crowd*, and his wife, Evie. My mother was a good friend of David's sister Mary. She had known her at Bryn Mawr. Nerys and Orlando Patterson lived in the next house to me. Orlando had just won the National Book Award. Nerys and I became great friends. She was a social anthropologist from Wales. She used to tell me the story of her family, which was very complicated and included English royalty. I believe she has written a memoir about it. She and Orlando had met at the London School of Economics. She returned to Wales to take care of her mother and to teach at the University of Wales. She came back to visit me and gave me a copy of her recently published book, *Cattle Lords and Clansmen*.

My neighbor behind me on Hudson Street was Elaine Kistiakowsky, the widow of the physicist. She was one of the most marvelous people I have ever met. She was active in local and state politics, and if you wanted *anything*, to know where "posslq" came from (the census: person of opposite sex, same living quarters), home grown red and yellow tomatoes from her place on the Cape, to cut back one of her lilac bushes, somewhere to go for Thanksgiving where you would meet not only city councilor Alice Wolf and her husband, but her husband's father—you had it. Alice Wolf was incredibly helpful to me about a situation in which I was harassed by construction workers next door, and I am no longer afraid to call the Cambridge police, who are in general very non-sexist and very good.

Elaine's husband, the chemist George Kistiakowsky, worked for the Army during the Korean War and he invented an explosive that one could also eat. It was called "Aunt Jemima." During the Vietnam War he became a dove and drove around in a VW painted all over with flowers and vines.

A friend of mine whom I had gone out with when we were both in graduate school had become the print curator at a southern university. He flew up to see me.

I wanted to go to a yard sale and he said he had never been to one. He ended up spending most of the day at yard sales and reappeared with a lot of hand made pots.

"Are you going to take those all back on the *plane* with you?" I asked. "How will you carry them?"

"Oh, somehow," he said. "I *like* them."

I said to him, "My mother used to say that the Germans were unspeakable, the French were superficial, and the English were *so silly*, and that was the highest compliment."

We met a couple of hours later in the Square for coffee before he left.

I was standing on Brattle Street waiting for him, and suddenly I saw him across the street. For a minute I didn't recognize him. His high, thin shoulders had broadened and he had filled out since graduate school days, and I was seeing him objectively now for the first time. He started to cross the street, and I heard the trumpets blow. That's the only time that's ever happened to me.

Chapter 20

But he had a little girl, Ellie, in the south and he had to go back.

We had had our relationship in graduate school, and I let it go this time. But we talked on the phone. About a year later he told me he was going to marry a woman he had known in high school. She lived in California, and he said he was going to move to California.

"*Don't*," I said. "*Don't leave Ellie.* You're connection with her will break, you won't have any daily life with her, and she'll feel you've betrayed her and she'll never trust anyone again. I have no right to tell you what to do, but that's my advice."

"I'll think about it very seriously," he said, and he didn't move to California.

When I first left teaching, I audited a course in Linguistics, which I had developed an interest in, at the Harvard Summer School. After class one day I met an Armenian non-Jewish Israeli philosophy student. I was thirty and he was twenty-one. He played the violin, and he said he couldn't live without seeing two movies a week. We had a lot to say to each other, including, imitating Woody Allen, "Are we going to have lunch, or *what?*," "Who am I supposed to be, fucking *Heisenberg*?" (me) when our affair was in uncertainties, and, when he asked me what I was thinking and I said, "There's not a thought in my mind," "Kierkegaard would not agree."

He was leaving for graduate school in Toronto in September. We had lunch.

"How can you *do* this to me?" I asked.

"How can I do *what* to you?" he said, surprised.

"Leave me here with all these *Americans*," I said.

I had had lunch with Hilary Putnam shortly before I left teaching. He had just returned from Israel. I asked him how it was.

"I feel safer there than I do in Boston," he said.

What It Isn't

Literature reveals life by showing what it isn't. The whiteness of the page, print and all, points up the colors of the world beside it. We read to lose life, and find it again, when we put the book down, heightened.

Peter said, as we came out of the Society of Fellows, "Reality!" He put his hand up to his face as a truck rolled by. "It's still here!"

"There's something very real about that corner," I said when we were safely past it. "Sometimes I've been just sitting in the living room of the Society, drinking coffee, and have come out and been overwhelmed right here by reality."

Peter grinned. "Maybe it's the coffee," he said. "Or," he continued as though he were saying something hackneyed which in this case might prove germane, "maybe it points out the *unreality* of the Society of Fellows."

"That's quite possible," I said.

The Society of Fellows had become my new home, and my new friends. I had nothing to do but paint and make prints, and the Society is where I hung out.

On my way home I stopped by a street vendor's cloth on the ground and bought a silver choker. "It's not real silver," the street vendor said, "but it's not junky metal. It won't turn your neck green." I tried it on in his mirror and liked it, and, thinking that I could not imagine a situation in which I would wear it, I bought it anyway. It reminded me of situations in which 1 might have worn it.

"It's starting to rain," he said.

"Don't get wet," I told him. He was my age and a throwback.

"Just a few drops," he offered, and I offered, "It's better than the heat wave we've had."

"It broke none too soon," he said seriously. "I thought that if it went on a day longer, there was going to be trouble."

"You're not kidding," I said.

"Well", he said, "They say we're never tested beyond our limits."

"Not true: all the time," I said, opting for the energetic approach.

be, fucking *Heisenberg*?" (me) 'Well, I'm only mouthing what they say," he said.

"Well," I said, "it's a nice idea. Don't get wet."

"Oh, no," he said, as the sky bulged. "I'm good at scurrying."

I went into the typist's as the drops quickened. I said, "Can I bring you some more typing?"

"Oh, sure," she said. "You brought me poems before, didn't you? That was nice."

"It's stories this time," I told her. "I'll bring them next week."

"I'll do them the week after," she said. "Next week I have mailing lists to do. It's starting to rain."

"I know," I said.

"I don't think it will amount to much," she said.

"It's pretty black outside," I said. "Well, thanks."

"Oh, that's okay," she said. "As long as it's nice for the weekend."

"Oh, it will be," I said. "Well, thanks a lot."

"Thank you," she said. "See you."

"Yup," I said.

The rain had stopped when I got outside and all the hoses were shattering the walks with spray.

The week before, Carrie and I had had lunch at The Tasty. My father ate there when he was in college. I gave her a birthday present and a post card of a gypsy standing in front of a sign saying, "Your loves, your desires, your future." Peter was away, and Carrie and I talked of love and life. Nowhere else in the Square is there a just plain hamburger place, stools and all. Carrie said she loved it and I said it was like New York. It was very real, compared to the nonexistence of the city around it, anyway. Later Peter, who is a physicist, asked me if I'd liked it, and I said it was too much reality for me. He asked in amusement, "Is that your notion of reality?" I told this to Jaklin, who said she had passed it that morning, taking a walk before sitting down to her thesis, and that she would have to go and see if it corresponded to her notion of reality. What that notion would be, Istanbul or Tel Aviv or linguistics, I have some idea, I realized, but not a clear one.

Still, after I'd come home and read all the magazines I'd bought to find places to send stories to, and after I'd thought of going out and decided that it was too much reality and that I'd take a nap, the story of the day appeared, set off by the white pages, the unreality of the magazines. In one of them I'd found a poem talking about exactly the same thing, about a song: "The metre / And the notes — black, false, and wrong. / But the lamb and the snow looked whiter: / The point of any old song."

I think the white page makes a red, a yellow reality, however false and wrong, where the page isn't. Literature is life, and the stories in the world beside the page are the stories. We wouldn't know that if we didn't drop into that nonexistent world now and then, where there is nothing, so that, coming out of the Society again, we can put our hands up to our faces and say, "Reality!"

It's really raining now.

21. THAT NIGHT

About four in the morning I woke up. I often woke up then in those days, and I wanted to get up and have some coffee, because there was no point in trying to go back to sleep: I was *awake*. I wanted to paint, but I was too tired. So I went into the kitchen and put the kettle on, and then, in the manic state of mind I often have at four in the morning, I decided to steam the t-shirts I had painted the day before, now that the paint would be dry. To steam them, I had to hang them, one at a time, on the curtain rod on the door onto the back porch. I proceeded to do so. I plugged in the little steamer, and I was drinking coffee and steaming away and trying not to knock anything off the counter with the cord, when I heard a noise on the porch.

It was still dark. It sounded like someone snoring.

It's my state of mind, I thought. I went on steaming.

Someone on the porch turned over and groaned.

Oh, no, I thought.

What with the hour and the coffee and my state of mind, I was petrified. Behind the t-shirt there was a curtain. I was afraid to lift it.

Well, I thought, I'll just stop steaming and go in the living room.

I went in the living room and drank my coffee. Then I began to get mad. Why should I be tiptoeing around like this?

Chapter 21

I hate to call the police. I really hate it. I came of age when the police came after you with tear gas in riot gear. But this isn't the 1960s any more, I told myself, and you don't know who's on the porch.

I called the police.

I stood in the kitchen, waiting, and pretty soon a police car pulled into the parking lot behind the house. I heard a man's voice yell, "All right, on your feet." Then I heard some kind of stumbling, tripping noises. I was paralyzed with terror. I couldn't look out.

"What are you doing here?" the man's voice yelled.

"Sleeping," said a little voice.

"Do you know the people who live here?" said the yell.

"Yeah," said the little voice.

"What's their name?"

"Nan," said the little voice.

"Nan *what*?"

I opened the porch door and screamed out hysterically, "Jeff! I didn't know it was you. Christ!"

"Do you know this guy?" the policeman asked dubiously.

"*Yes*," I said. "Jesus, Jeff, you idiot, you scared me to death."

I'd had it. I went in and shut the door. I heard the police car take off. I knew the front doorbell would ring soon.

It rang. I opened the door. Jeff stumbled in. I was shaking.

"Christ," he said. He was still half asleep.

"I didn't know it was you," I said. I was half crying. Policemen scare me to death.

"I know," he said, alert to the situation through what I could tell was a gallon of liquor.

"*Why didn't you wake me up?*" I screamed.

"I didn't want to disturb you," he said. He smiled. "What were you doing up at five in the morning?"

"Steaming t-shirts," I said.

We sat down on the sofa. He'd obviously been terrified by the lights and the yelling. "They had guns," he said.

"What did they say?" I asked.

"They said if they ever picked me up again they'd put me in the joint. They were pretty nice to me. They just drove me around the block. Oh God, am I wasted."

I was supposed to sing at a coffeehouse benefit for the homeless at the Old Cambridge Baptist Church that night. I'd never sung before an audience, only on the street in Harvard Square. I really wanted to do it. I had to stay cool.

"Shit," Jeff said. "Shit."

I put my arm around him, more for my sake than for his. I felt as though I might fly into a million pieces, or drop dead.

"I hadn't had a drink since I got out of the rehab center," said Jeff. "But tonight's the anniversary of Rikki's suicide, and the guys offered me free drinks, and I just didn't care." I could see that he didn't.

We talked. It got lighter outside. "My whole life," Jeff kept saying. "My whole life."

"Vietnam killed you," I said. I was falling to pieces and there was nothing to hold on to.

"I never *done* nothing," he said.

We both cried. "If you marry that guy," Jeff said, "which I doubt."

I had two hearts, and they were pulling me apart.

I had nothing, not one thing, left to give. We'd peeled out, I'd laid all the rubber, and I was riding on the rim.

When it was light, Jeff walked out into the morning.

It seemed as though already it was time to go to the coffee house. I had to do it. Sometimes I function best when I'm the most out of it.

I took a taxi because it was raining and I didn't want my guitar to get wet.

There was a small crowd, but it got bigger. I sat frozen in a corner, watching my anxiety.

The performers were pretty good. There was a young woman in hip boots who wrote her own songs, and an elderly gay in white shorts and a pith helmet who seemed to be a local fixture and who sang "Mack the Knife." He was amazing. "Camp," someone yelled. "What?" someone called. "High camp," they yelled back.

Then the emcee called my name. I'd figured out that I couldn't walk up those steps to the stage, that I would have to sit on the edge of it. The mike guy was very nice and arranged the mikes on the floor.

I sang the songs I was most used to, my father's songs, "The Water Is Wide," and

> Au quatre coins du lit
> Coulent des fleuves profondes.
> Nous resterons ici
> Jusqu'a la fin du monde, jusqu'a la fin du monde.

My father said that wasn't the way it went, but that's how I remember his singing it, after my parents had split up and we all lived in New York, where all of this should have been happening but wasn't. What were we all doing here, anyway? It was getting dark. We should have gone home long ago.

22. THE LAST HAPPY MAN

My new love, Emil, the antithesis to Jeff, kept me company through three months of a burned foot. Now my foot was well.

I was in love as though with my childhood sweetheart. Emil was brilliant, witty, from New York, knew art and literature; I had found my past. Emil's father knew Matisse, Noel Coward, Marlene Dietrich, well. I was at home at last. And Emil saw Roosevelt drive by Washington Square.

My childhood sweetheart said that crying was the therapy. I told him of the chapter in *The Tin Drum* about the onion cellar, where after the war people in Germany who can no longer cry, and who *have* to cry, go in the evenings to peel onions and cry. He said that in the Middle Ages they cried, they didn't have penicillin, they just cried, that that was how they survived. I said I thought that crying was good but laughing was better.

As Groucho says in *Duck Soup*, when he steps out of the sidecar after Harpo has driven furiously off without him, and surveys his presidential palace, "It's good to be home again." The story of everyone's life.

Dear God, I loved him so.

I hadn't loved anyone this way since my teddy bear. Teddy. Completely trustworthy. Infinite sympathy. Unconditional love. Steadfast to the end. Innuendo is your beginning.

Chapter 22

When Mistletoe was a baby she used to stare at an electrical outlet with a plug in it above her crib.

"Why does she stare at it?" my mother asked me.

"It's a face," I said. "It's a face saying 'Awkestra.'"

I had a bushel basket full of cars and trucks, Abigail and Sign Go and Handsome Nervous Pickle Tin. I knew the make and year of every car on the block. One day I called to my mother, "Mummy, come quick! The baby looks like the new Oldsmobile!"

My mother was cooking and saying an animal for every letter of the alphabet. "And I is for—I can't think what I is for. I is for ibis, but I don't know what an ibis is.

I was about eighteen months. "Mumma!" I said. "A ibis is a heron!"

My grandfather remembered that I walked into a living room full of people at about that age and asked, "Are all these people mathematicians?"

My mother and I were having tea in tiny toy teacups, I was telling her all about my family. Mistletoe was sitting in her playpen

Finally my mother said, "And who is that?"

"Oh, that's me hisband's mither."

My mother told me that I used to quote A.A. Milne, "There was a rawing in the 'ky." My father always said "sundertorm," as I had said it. My mother loved thunderstorms, and in Randolph we used to go out on the lawn and dance around in them at night. We used to lie out in deck chairs and watch shooting stars and the *aurora borealis*.

I asked my father last year why the video game was called Nintendo. "I don't know," he said. I said, "I always thought it was, 'Didn't intendo no innuendo.'" "I thought it was an apology: 'Nintendo—I didn't mean to,'" he said. "Oh," I said, "and children play it and they feel better." "Por favor, signor, Nintendo drop the soup in your lap," my father burst out with delight.

My mother, the complete book, three thousand miles and three thousand years away, loved that.

I was drawing a pastel portrait of my half-brother Seth. My father said, "I'd give my little finger to be able to do that."

When the print curator at the Fogg bought one of my etchings, I told Emil that I came rushing out into the lobby in my homemade cotton dress and long hair and told the guard, who had a pony tail—Emil bristled—that the Fogg had just bought one of my prints, and that he had said, "A shooting star, that's what you are." Emil laughed. My father was so jealous that he said, "Why don't you change your name to Fogg? I think there was a mathematician named Fogg."

"Phineas Fogg," I said.

"*Phileas* Fogg," he said.

My father was extremely radical when he was young. He never talked about it, except once to say to me, "It's very difficult for someone like me who belonged to the John Reed Club," a student Communist club at Harvard in the 1930s, "to accept what happened in the Soviet Union."

He said this at a time when he was very active in getting Jewish mathematicians and scientists out of the Soviet Union. One Easter Sunday in New York a family arrived from Moscow. My father had arranged for them to stay in a vacant apartment of a friend near him on the Upper West Side. He and I went over there. Grigory Chudnovsky had myasthenia gravis. He was lying in bed. His father had been beaten up by the KGB at the Moscow airport. We couldn't get a doctor on Easter Sunday in New York. Mama Chudnovsky kept offering me an orange and three chocolates, all the food there was in the house. Grigory's brother David was rushing around trying to look out for everyone.

My father and I sat by Grigory's bed. My father and he talked about literature for two hours. Grigory was almost too weak to move. He was emaciated, with dark hair and a dark beard and high cheekbones. He was luminous, like a Christ. "Exactly like something out of Dostoievski," my father said later. Eventually my father got him into his wheelchair and took him out for a walk. Mama kept offering me chocolates. Grigory's father was shut in his bedroom. The KGB had hit him in the liver.

"Isn't he something?" my father said about Grigory as we left. "He's *me*."

Grigory and David were mathematicians. My father found them jobs. He and they arranged for a great symposium in New York in honor of the Soviet dissident physicist Sakharov. Sakharov sent a paper, and David and others gave papers. The auditorium was packed. Mama Chudnovsky was there. My father had had a poster designed for the occasion, and it was being sold to raise money for Sakharov.

The *New Yorker* later published an article about the Chudnovskys. My father was interviewed in it.

In about 1983 I was having an exhibition in Cambridge, and my father was coming up for the opening. The daughter of Elena Bonner, Sakharov's wife, Tanya Yankelevich, and her husband were just arriving in Newton. My father suggested that I invite them, and I did. Tanya Yankelevich came, and she and my father talked for about an hour. She was trying to get through to Elena Bonner to say that they had made it safely to America.

I met a Russian Jewish émigré pianist, Helena Vesterman. We became quite close. She had been a well-known concert pianist in the Soviet Union and had emigrated because she didn't want her two young sons to grow up under Communism and anti-Semitism. She had piano recitals at her apartment in Brooklyn. I called Emmanuel Boroch, who had helped many Russian refuge musicians, but he said that there were too many to help.

My father said, "Well, you have your émigré and I have mine."

Helena gave me Russian lessons. I had discovered the Russian poet Marina Tsvetaeva and was trying to do some translations. I told Helena how much I loved her.

"She's *your* poet," Helena said.

The Last Happy Man

My father's middle name was Ellis, for Ellis Island.

My father was very close to Robert Gorham Davis and his wife, Hope Hale Davis, in the 30s. It was Hope who, in the 1980s, over a lunch of baked beans and cottage cheese in their Cambridge apartment, told me about my father's political activism during that time. Later I had dinner with Hope and Robert and Robert talked about his political relationship with my father a great deal. Hope taught a course in memoir writing at the Radcliffe Institute. She was 100. When I showed her the parts of this manuscript that talked about my father as a parent, she said that she thought that it was wonderful to have a world famous mathematician shown that way. After my father died, she said that she remembered having lunch with us at Butler Hall at Columbia in the 1950s and being impressed by how affectionate and admiring he was toward us children. "You'll always have that," she said.

Recently I said to a friend of mine from Little Hollow, "No matter how awful that place was, it's left me with one thing. I still see the world as a radical community."
My friend is a neoconservative. "So do I," he said.
Way back, it was my father who saw the world as a radical community. He lived his politics. He talked to everyone: people in grocery stores, Aldous Huxley for hours in the Museum of Modern Art, Stieglitz in his studio for years, the women in his life — wealthy divorcees and hardworking editors and women of all professions whom he would take us to see after "The Fantasticks" or "My Fair Lady," to show us off. He took me to hear Alicia de la Roche and during the applause he took my hand and we walked up onto the stage and he introduced me to her. He introduced me to Rosalind Turek. He knew Woody Guthrie. He told me that he

thought that the great heroes of the age were Allen Ginsberg and Bob Dylan.

When my friend Ellen and I went to France one summer when I was in graduate school, my father said, "You have to look up Elizabeth!" and wrote down a telephone number. So when I got to Paris I called Elizabeth.

"I'm Herbert Robbins' daughter," I said.

"You *must* come over for lunch," Elizabeth said.

I found the house. It was like a palace. It had a courtyard. Elizabeth greeted me and the nanny came in with the two children, a boy and a girl, impeccably and beautifully dressed. We sat down to lunch, which was brought in by the cook. For desert there was hand made orange sherbet in orange rinds.

After lunch Elizabeth threw herself down on the sofa.

"Now," she said, "*whose* daughter did you say you are?"

"Herbert Robbins,'" I said.

"*Herbert Robbins*!" she said. "He took a splinter out of my foot on the train from Washington to New York!"

"I did," said my father, when I reported this story to him.

Ellen and I went to Dinard and called Nicole Plevin, who was an old friend of my parents and whose sister Francoise's gallery had designed the poster for the Sakharov symposium. She was having company and couldn't see us, but Ellen and I danced on the beach at Dinard during a thunderstorm.

Once, years after my parents were divorced, my father found himself in the neighborhood of my grandfather's summer home, which was part of a club that was restricted from Jews. He dropped in on them for tea. They were amazed, but glad to see him. "Why not?" he said to me. When I was thinking about doing something new or interesting, he would always say, "Why not?"

My father loved my mother's mother, and when she died, he was the first to send flowers. My grandfather was amazed.

In the 1960s, my father did the demographics for the first congressional campaign of Elizabeth Holtzman, congresswoman from Brooklyn, who later sat on the judiciary Committee during the Watergate hearings. For Statistica, my father's company, my father testified for women who were bringing discrimination suits against universities and colleges when they were denied tenure. In the 1980s he said to me, "All jobs should be given to Blacks and women for twenty years." I expressed surprise and admiration. "How else are you going to do it?" he asked.

When Anwar Sadat, the president of Egypt who was later assassinated for doing so, made peace with Israel, he came to speak at the United Nations in New York. My father admired him so much that he went to the Columbia Book Store and bought a Columbia necktie and sent it in a taxi out to the airport to Sadat when he was leaving for Egypt, with a note. Sadat wrote him a letter thanking him for the tie, and my father had it framed and hung it over his desk.

He also had framed and hung over his desk a document from the International Star Registry with a star named after him. I had ordered it for him.

"I wonder what the schools are like up there," he said wistfully.

My father's work made statistical methods applicable to almost any practical problem: drug trials—he worked for NIH; insurance. When he died I got a sympathy card from an editing client who said that he was a cement layer and he had used my father's methods to figure out how much cement he needed to fill a given space.

On August 4, 1985, the *New York Times Book Review* published a letter I had written, under the heading, "The 1960s Defended":

To the Editors,

In Annie Gottlieb's review of Abe Peck's book "Uncovering the Sixties," (July 7), she describes the style of the book as "strangely unsubstantial—like the 1960s themselves." It might be well to remember that we are looking at the 1960s from a decade that is itself strangely unsubstantial. The issues in the 1960s were at least clear: most people agreed that there was a war going on and that there was virulent racial discrimination in this country. The antiwar and desegregation efforts of the 1960s reached some of their goals. It remains for similar efforts to have as substantial an impact today. To reject the 1960s on the basis of "style" leads precisely to the reaction and repression of the 1980s. It is at least faulty hindsight, at most fear of the power they contained, that makes us see the 1960s as fantasy rather than as a cogent reality we must incorporate as part of our past if we are to move forward into anything but disaster.

My father called me up in delight.
"A whole generation defended!" he said.

Once I called my father,
"Are you surrounded by friends?" he asked.
"There's no one here," I said.
"Well, there's no one here," he said. Then he said, "But that's impossible! No one can't be in two places at the same time." He paused. "I like that," he said, sounding pleased.

My father was interviewed on television by Walter Cronkite. It was the last program in a series. My father was talking about the possibility of nuclear war. "Einstein said, 'God does not play dice,'" my father said, "I think God is playing dice with *us!*"
I called my father to congratulate him. "End of program, end of series, end of world!" he said jubilantly.
When my father was dying, he said, "I want to see the fireworks!"

When my father was dying, he quoted T. S. Eliot to me: "Time present and time past/Are present in time future."

My mother used to say that often, and she added the next line: "And time future in time present."

She used to quote Einstein, when he was asked how he felt when a colleague of his died: "This death signifies nothing. Past, present, and future are all happening at once. Time is an illusion, although a stubborn one."

It's not "precognition." It's all happening at the same time.

This is all ye need to know on earth, and all ye need to know.

This is the afterlife.

It's like Fellini's movie, "8 1/2." It doesn't matter, because it's all happening at the same time, and it's a circle.

My mother used to say that when Einstein was asked where he got all these things, like $E=MC^2$, he said, "From my imagination."

I was talking about everything.

"It's just a dream," my father said.

When my father was dying, he said, "People are interchangeable."

This is the cardinal sin. It's the thing you're not supposed to say. People are supposed to be *irreplaceable*. If you think they're not, it's something called "transference."

But people *are* interchangeable, thank God.

I thought my father should know. As I said to him once when he was depressed and he said, "Oh, it's all come to nothing," "How can you say that? You have more children and more wives than anyone in the world."

Once we were all at the beach and there was Daniel at the water's edge looking exactly like Mistletoe at three, and I said to my father, "Do you have a distinct sense of *deja vu*?" and he said, "Oh, I'm totally confused." Then he got in an inner tube and paddled around for an hour, looking at us on the shore all the time and looking more pleased with himself than anyone I've ever seen.

My father knew that people are interchangeable. This was why Mistletoe was so amazed that he was interested in *everything*, when he came out to Seattle to see her and began talking to an old

Chapter 22

man on a bus who had been to a ceramics show, the way he used to talk to Stieglitz and everyone else. Mistletoe said that she thought of my father as sitting with his head in his hands in utter depression. Sometimes he did, especially, my mother said, at parties. But the next minute he would be whistling.

My father's family had two dogs, Raskolnikov and Phoebe. They were his life. In the spring I had phoebes all around my house. I told my father, "They whistle 'Phoebe. Phoebe.'"

They didn't have them in Princeton. "I *wish* I could hear them," my father said.

I still hear them.

My father's best-known work was called "empirical Bayes." I said to him, "Isn't there someone in your professional life named Bayes?"

"Bayes, yes," he said.

"Well, listen to this," I said. "'The Garden,' by Andrew Marvell. It's got you both in the same poem.

> How vainly men themselves amaze
> To win the palm, the oak, or *bays*,
> And their incessant labors see
> Crowned by some single *herb*, or tree.

"My heavens!" said my father. "Well, what do you know?"

When my father was seventy-five he was honored by the mayor of New York and given the keys to the city.

I sent him a card on which I had typed, a la the *New Yorker*.

> The Following Item Is Reprinted in its Entirety

> Robbins found by a reporter
> To have a remarkable daughter.
> When asked, "Do you find
> Some kinship of mind?"

Robbins told the reporter, "Well, sorter."

"I liked your *New Yorker* item," my father said. "Cute."

I sent him a cartoon entitled "An Evening with Andre Breton," in which Breton is seen from the back standing raging and waving his fists in the air and saying, "Whom do I haunt?" and his girlfriend is sitting at a little table in the foreground with a glass, looking completely fucked over, and saying, "Nobody, Andre. Relax."

"Cute," said my father. "Send it to the *New Yorker*."

In the 1980s I started publishing poems in little magazines. I showed them all to my father.

My father said, "You're the part of me that escaped."

My father told me to read a biography by Mary McCarthy, *Rachel Varnagen*. "It's about *you*," he said.

I read it, and I was surprised that he thought that it was about me. It's about a terribly emotional woman caught up in and misguided by the social and political currents of her day.

"Did you understand it?" my father asked.

"No," I said.

He said, "It's one long scream."

" Why does she remind you of me?" I asked.

"On second thought, she doesn't remind me at all of you," he said.

"She's awfully *pathetic*. I don't think I'm *quite* that pathetic."

" I don't think you're at *all* pathetic," said my father.

When we lived in Chapel Hill, in the late 1940s and early 1950s, we first lived in Victory Village, housing for professors and graduate students at the University of North Carolina, and their families. Victory Village was composed of barracks and cardboard houses that had been made to send to Britain. We lived in one of these houses. It was about 12' by 12', with an icebox—the iceman brought a block of ice each week—and a kerosene stove. It had four rooms, and in the beginning no telephone: there was a phone booth at the end of the street. All the houses on Johnson Street were like it.

"That was my favorite time," I said to my father.

"Mine, too," he said.

"That house was child sized," I said.

"You couldn't find a better house," he said. "I'd like one to put in the backyard, to study in."

I played with Australian and Canadian children. After my sister was born we bought the house at 413 Smith Avenue. Both of our houses were always full of mathematicians from all over the world—India, Japan, China, Israel, Russia—and also of American women mathematicians. In the housing project at the Institute for Advanced Study, my friends were Japanese and Australian children. The eminent mathematician Hassler Whitney, who was a champion roller skater, taught me to roller skate.

In Chapel Hill we had Black women who helped my mother take care of us children. One of them told her, "All the children walk along the road and play together, and then, when it's time for them to go into the first grade, some go one fork and some go another, and no one knows why."

My first political memory is of Orville Faubus, the segregationist governor of Arkansas.

When I walked into the classroom at 9 o'clock my first morning as an assistant professor and saw those Black faces, I felt as though I had come home.

My father said that he thought that Sherlock Holmes was the greatest character ever created. When I was a child he gave me *The Complete Sherlock Holmes* and I read it all until I came to the last story, and then I couldn't bear to have it come to an end, so I put the back flap in to save the place and put it away and didn't read it until I was in my forties.

The Last Happy Man

... My childhood sweetheart says that the crying is the therapy.
I often think that I am the happiest person in the world.
My father said, "I think we are witnessing the end of Western civilization as we know it."
My father once said: "I think I am the Last Happy Man."
The house was off of Gnarled Hollow Road. "Wonderful name," my father said. My twelve-year-old half-brother, in whom I have complete trust, bone of my bone, flesh of my flesh, and I went for a walk and in the tangled growth beside the road I spotted a gourd. "Oh, *look*," I said. "Do you want that?" he asked. A friend of mine at college said of a place where she liked to walk, "It's so *ingrown* in there." My half-brother climbed into the tangle and emerged with the gourd and gave it to me. He put his hands on his hips and looked exactly like my father. "Are you *happy*?"

My father's family was from the part of Russia that is now Poland.
We were eating dinner at his house on Long Island, during the time that all of Central Europe was rising up against Communism and demanding democracy. There were terrible food shortages.
"There's so much *food*," I said.
My father said, "This isn't Hungary."
As we drove to Central Islip Airport so I could get the plane home, we passed house after house with mattresses laid out on the curb.
"What is going *on*?" my father said. Then he said, "They're obeying Christ's injunction."
"What?" I said.
He said, "Pick up your beds and walk."
At the small airport, which we had sat in and waited so many times in plastic chairs, and which had what my college roommate used to call "a sense of placelessness," my father said, "I think this is Hungary."

Chapter 22

In the cab driving through the dark outskirts of Cambridge, I thought of New York and all that had passed since we left it, and of the great Russian émigré poet Joseph Brodsky's line,
"Leningrad, my telephone numbers are in your keeping!"

23. YARD SALE

I think of writing as a sort of yard sale. Old emotions, used emotions, emotions held in common. Yard sales are an important social phenomenon. They ease the pain of not knowing what to do with all that past, and they contribute to the general good. They are a way of saying, "I have known this. It is trustworthy. I pass it on to you." And you have the extraordinary excitement of having what is old, once more, without the fear.

Yard sales are not a stranger at your door bringing something never seen before which you may or may not want. They are not frightening. You *want* the past. You hope, when you go to a yard sale, to find the past, and you do.

Sometimes it is hard for writers to convey warmth, generosity of spirit. That's why it's important that there be yard sales. You can air your dirty linen in public, and people will say, "Oh, yes, this is lovely." You can be sure of finding a good home for your mother's guilt. You can be certain of discovering your father.

The usefulness and worth of your feelings are clear to everyone. They are worn and comfortable. They are just what we like. They are lovely. You need no longer have any doubts about them. "Oh, that's *great*," people say. "We *need* them. We can use them."

At yard sales you find the expected in the unexpected, and the unexpected in the expected. It's a little like ours, but different. We haven't seen one of these in years. That's just what we wanted.

And you have the guarantee that someone else has used it before you. It isn't so outlandish. Or so expensive.

People are very happy at yard sales. They are sure of getting something useful, for it has been used before. Yard sales are a sharing of the wealth of common human feelings. They are a giving of yourself to others. And we are appreciative. Yard sales are a relief from the dangers and loneliness of shopping. They make everything simple. People reach their hands into the piles and throw the clothes up in the air. They hold something up to themselves in delight. Oh, will it fit? They are freed from the formality and constraint of forbidding new clothes. They see a sure thing. And it is not theirs alone. It was someone else's too.

Yard sales are different from second hand shops. At a yard sale, you *know* whom things belong to. There is the instant, intimate communication of giving. There is fun, humility, embarrassment, and satisfaction. You take the things home with you and you are relieved not to have all that responsibility of being alone. You have received your mother's guilt all over again, but sweetened through having been used by someone else. It's new, and yet it's the same. That's why yard sales are perfect. And finding your father is no longer frightening. It is merely desired. These things are desired. I give them to you. You find your desires in others'. What you like is likeable, what you love, loveable. And loveable for having been loved.

I heard Isaac Bashevis Singer read, years ago, and I talked to him afterwards. All I had with me was a copy of *Richard II*, and I asked him to sign it. He signed it "Shakespeare II." He was so sweet, so loveable. "I would have hugged him," I said to a friend, "but he looked as though plenty of people had hugged him." This is the quality we're searching for.

Yeats' "foul rag and bone shop of the heart" becomes a tremendous yard sale, from which you return to yourself more yourself than you were. There is no great yard sale in the sky. Yard sales are an earthly phenomenon, tasting of tears, and tasting also of something deliciously sweet, a sense of perpetual recovery, the thing we have in common, the goodness and freshness of being.

24. "OLD MEN SHOULD BE EXPLORERS"

"I was naïve," Emil said, "then I became urbane."

He had studied history at Harvard and then gone to the Columbia School of Journalism. He had worked as an editor for Unesco-Paris, and had known everyone at the BBC and all the *New Yorker* writers. He had written four books on art, mostly published by Abrams. I thought he was like the world, the globe. 'I am a little world made cunningly.'

"I'd like to see Jerusalem," I said to him once.

"You *would?*" he asked with bated breath.

I was forty-two and Emil was just turning fifty. We were the only people we could talk to. We said everything, nursery rhymes. Both our lives were coming back.

Emil's father had been an artist. He had taught at the Art Students League. He had been on the fringe of the New York art circle in the 1950s. Emil had known Walkowitz, Trajan, Bazeotis. He knew everybody's widow. My mother had been an editor in New York before she got married, and after the divorce she had studied at the Art Students League. She was a wonderful artist. Her teacher, Howard Trafton, said to her, "All you have to do for the rest of your life is draw."

"We're closer to death than most people," Emil said to me once.

Chapter 24

When I first knew him, he said to me, "I love rain. I hate beautiful days."

"They're a terrible strain," I said.

He looked at me as though he suddenly began to know me.

"I hate it when it stays light late," he said.

"It's terribly sad," I said.

I had a dream that we were getting married and all the different classroom buildings and Memorial Church in Harvard Yard were churches of different denominations, each with its appropriate white cross outside.

Emil's parents had died, he had left Paris and London to come to Cambridge with a woman, he had left her, taught for a while, done another art book, and then he had sold his Matisses and Picassos and was working on a novel. He also got a very fancy Mac and began doing computer art. His father's aunt had supported his father's painting—his father was on the fringe of the New York circle in the 1950s, and Emil knew them all, or their widows—and Emil's aunt was supporting his writing and his art. Emil was completely intuitive. Most of our relationship was about money, and what not to do with it. Emil couldn't balance his checkbook to save his life. He would go down to the bank, and there would be nothing in his account, and there would be no way to figure out what had happened or to straighten it out.

I made my own clothes. I loved it. I would buy curtains, or beautiful batiks, at yard sales, and make dresses, sewing by hand. I took them to stores, and they wanted to buy them. Emil came over one day when I was finishing a dress.

"You make your own clothes?" he asked in amazement.

"Yes," I said. "I love it."

"That's happy," Emil said.

He asked me to make him a black wool cloak.

"Oh, I couldn't make something like that," I said. "Really. I don't know how to make button holes or anything. I'd need a machine. I wouldn't know how to fit you. Really, don't ask me to do it. I don't know how to make that kind of thing."

He was terribly offended. He went into Boston to a very expensive tailor and had him make him a long black wool cloak. He wore it all the time, around Harvard Square. He looked like something out of "The Phantom of the Opera."

"I know," I said, when he was berating himself about the bill. "You had to do it. Sometimes you have to spend money just to prove that you're alive."

"You said it," he said.

His aunt was in Florida, and he had another aunt and a cousin in Florida. He said one of his relatives used to refer to "your cousin Florida."

"It's like Shakespeare," I said. "Somebody said that Shakespeare was all 'Get thee to Essex, Wessex. Get thee to Norfolk, Suffolk."

He was constantly troubled by his relatives, their ways, their manners, their professions. They all had names of flowers.

"You have a herbaceous border of relatives," I said.

He couldn't understand them. They weren't like his parents, especially his mother, whom he had adored.

Once we were talking about Horowitz.

"Everybody should be Horowitz," I said.

"Yes," he said. "Everybody should be Horowitz."

Emil asked me who my favorite poet was.

"Tennyson," I said.

"Really?" he cried. "Good for you."

I recited "The Splendour Falls" to him.

"That's my favorite poem," I said.

"That's your favorite poem?" he cried in amazement.

Emil thought that Shelley's "The Cloud" was fantastic.

It is.

One day we were having lunch in a restaurant and talking about Yeats.

"You see the images through the music," I said.

"It's true," he said.

I began reciting "A Prayer for My Daughter":

Chapter 24

> For many a poor man who has roved,
> Loved, and thought himself beloved,
> From a glad kindness cannot take his eyes.

My own eyes filled with tears as I said it.
Emil was startled.
"I'll look it up," he said softly.

I never drink, but one night I had a glass of sherry and I called Emil.
"I've made a lot of mistakes in my life," I said, "and I intend to make a lot more before I'm through."
I called him back.
"I'm sorry," I said. "Was I terrible?"
"No," he chuckled. "It was wonderful."

I think Emil and I loved each other very much, better than life or death. It was terribly difficult, and it made me very practical to deal with his problems, which was very good for me, and even took me away from him a little. But it was a spiritual love, and I thirsted for him and felt my thirst quenched by him the way people feel about spiritual things.

I remember being in a shoe store, and hearing Yves Montand singing, "Ne quitte moi," and I will never forget it.

I felt, underneath all the practicalities, something rising within me. I used to sing in Harvard Square, songs we both knew, "It's Very Clear," and I knew that I knew what love was for the first time.

Emil was old fashioned, even more so than my father. He seemed to be of my grandfather's generation. We used to talk about politics—I was much more radical than he was—and he would say something, and then he would say, "I think that's balanced," and it was.

"I'm not doctrinaire," I said to him once.
"No," he murmured. "I know you're not."

Once, when we were having a particularly difficult time, I told him that I had gotten a letter from a left wing editor signed, "Yours in the struggle" (Emil sounded annoyed) and that I had been so honored, and that after that I had dreamt that I was talking to Emil and had sat straight up in bed and said aloud to him, "Yours in the struggle."

"I think that's the most touching thing I've ever done," I said.

"Oh, no," he said. "I don't think so."

I thought of once when I first knew him and I simply put my arms around him on the street, and he stroked my long hair. He was so gentle, you trusted him implicitly.

When Communism fell, Emil told me with great delight that the headline across the front page of the *Boston Herald* was "THE PARTY'S OVER."

"We have so many freedoms that they don't have," he said.

I walked out in the clear, light, summer evening to rent a video. A few other people were walking along Massachusetts Avenue. It was perfectly peaceful and quiet, and I could see all the way up the avenue.

"You're right," I told him.

Emil was not always so gentle when he was drinking. I would call him up and he would try to scare me, screaming, and I would be afraid only because he was afraid. He lived at 21 Ellery Street, where Delmore Schwartz had lived.

"What does Emil like to do?" asked my mother on the phone from Seattle.

"He likes to moan and groan and clank his chains," I said.

She laughed.

"Really," I said.

"Somebody asked, 'Is it better to be loved because of things or in spite of things?'" I said to him.

"Oh, in spite of things," he said.

Emil had asked me early in our relationship whether I had ever seen a movie called *The Ghost and Mrs. Muir*. I hadn't, but at some point I saw it on TV. It's about a woman who rents a haunted house and falls in love with the ghost. He tries to spook her with roaring and thunder and lightning, but she loves him, and eventually she dies and then they can be together.

I told Emil that I had seen it.

"Oh, that's *wonderful*," he said, as if it meant everything to him.

I didn't know what it meant then, but I do now.

Emil had known S.J. Perelman in London. S.J. Perelman was interested in mysticism, and he had gotten Emil interested in it. Emil said that once they had been in a room together and Emil had spoken his dead father's name. There was a *crack!* and a rose broke in half. "Roses don't break like that," Emil said to me.

Emil believed in lots of things—astrology, the tarot. He believed that the spirits of his parents could help him in crises. "Spirit help," he called it.

"We're all very complicated people," he said to me once.

Once I was blue and angry and Emil said, "Never take yourself seriously."

"I never took myself seriously," said my father on the phone. "I never took myself seriously!"

"In New York," Emil said, "You collapse in front of Tiffany's. In Boston you just Shreve, Crump and Low."

Professor John Finley at Harvard used to call the Cambridge opticians Montgomery, Frost, and Lloyd, Montgomery, Lost, and Freud.

Emil and I were having lunch in a café. It was always a question whether we would sleep together. Emil confessed to me that he had gotten "a two in computation." He had gone to The High School of Music and Art in New York.

"A two out of ten?" I asked.

"A two out of a hundred," he said, "And that was because I put my name on the paper."

"The only things that ever bothered me were word problems," I said. "If A starts digging a ditch at the rate of two feet an hour, and

B starts digging at the other end at three feet an hour, when can they sit down and have lunch?"

"She was too young to go so far. He was too old to go so fast. How long would it take them to get to Turin in a Ferrari?" Emil sang out.

I thought this was the wittiest thing I'd ever heard. I told it to my father, the mathematician. He was flabbergasted.

"As a *word problem*?" he asked.

Emil had written a booklet of puns, such as, "She was poeming around the house. 'Will he ever come to me?' she thought. Byron by he did."

I thought they were wonderful, and I started writing them. "Suddenly he wanted to put his Brahms around her. 'My God,' he thought, 'I'm Smetana!'"

I told one to Emil over lunch. "A man is telling his skiing exploits. He says, 'I've skied Mount Everest,' and so on. His listener doesn't believe him, and he says, 'Well, that's very impressive, but tell me, did you ever rim ski?'"

"Korsakov!" Emil bellowed.

One night I called Emil and he was drinking and talking about "*veritas*." He was trying to close the refrigerator door. He would talk, and then there would be a *thump*, and he would keep talking, and then there would be another *thump*. Finally, *thump*, and, "Ah, I got it," he said with relief.

"What was wrong with it?" I asked.

"There were newspapers stuck in the bottom of the door," he said.

I loved him completely.

"I think things seem very simple to you," I said once.

"Yes," he said, "they do."

But they weren't simple at all.

I said to my father, "I'm writing a memoir called 'Earth and Air and Fire and Water.'"

"Ooh," he said. "That's what the Greeks thought the universe was made of, isn't it?"

"Yes," I said.

About the same time I woke up at 2 a.m. from a dream that someone was hacking my mother to death in her apartment. It was only 11 p.m. in Seattle, so I called her.

"Oh, no, dear," she said, "I'm defrosting the refrigerator, and I was just thinking, 'Any one passing in the hall will know what this hacking noise is.'"

"Well, you didn't think it soon enough," I said.

When Emil was diagnosed with cancer, we both knew that he might kill himself.

"If you killed yourself, it would be the end of me," I said.

I couldn't think of any other argument.

"No, it wouldn't," he said in surprise.

"Yes, it *would*," I said.

"No, it wouldn't," he said.

"Yes, it *would*," I said.

He looked at me oddly, and he didn't kill himself.

I had lunch with Emil shortly before he was diagnosed with cancer. It was the only time I have ever seen a Ruin. It did something strange to me.

I was working on a book about relationships among the Impressionists with a woman art historian. I ran my own editorial service. I was also studying printmaking and painting very seriously, and had been for about twenty years. I had had thirty shows in the Boston and New York areas, and I had published my book of poems and etchings, *Amelie*, with Ommation Press. I gave a copy to William Sloane Coffin when he spoke at a church near Harvard

Square. I had prints in the Loeb Art Center at Vassar, the Fogg Museum, and the Smith College Museum of Art.

The woman art historian was very close to Meyer Schapiro, and we finished the manuscript by their joint birthday, when she was going to see him. It was a rush, and I sent him a monotype with "And shall Jerusalem be builded here" written on it. When she came back she told me that he had loved it, and she brought me photos of him because ever since I had first seen him I had wanted to do a portrait of him, but I have never done it.

A couple of weeks later Emil called. "I have a sore throat and a lump," he said. "I'm too anxious to leave the house." He sounded terrible. Both of his parents had died young of cancer, and it was all he could think about, all the time.

"It's probably a swollen gland," I said. "Meet me at Au Bon Pain."

I went. I waited. After about an hour he showed up. He was delirious, wandering around the tables, talking to himself. He sat down.

"Where is it?" I asked.

"On my neck."

I looked at his neck. There was a lump on the left side.

I put my finger on it. At that moment I grew up.

"Is this it?" I asked.

"Yes."

"Does it hurt?"

"Yes."

"Go to the Walk-in Clinic at Mount Auburn," I said. He had been there before, both with me, when I had my burnt foot debrided—he was the only person I would have trusted to go with me, though I hardly knew him then—there was a deep well of trust for him—I trusted him more than any person I had ever met the moment I saw him—and by himself.

After I had had my foot debrided, when Emil and I were going home in a taxi, I took his hand, and he said, "Where are your parents?"

I understood what he meant.

Chapter 24

Emil sat there talking to himself for half an hour. Then he said, "All right."

"Go *now*," I said.

"All right."

He was the color of plate glass.

The room was from Paris, an apartment on the back, away from the Cambridge street. Soft, dull light filtered through the gold curtain. It had the infinite distance of a desert. Dust and sand and perfect quiet, like a picture without depth.

"It's another dimension, without time or space," I cried.

"You said it," Emil answered.

A great migration of things had begun inward, toward some magnetic pole, like white, frozen electricity charging back to its source. Elaborate things had come from him, like Klimt paintings, with elaborate exteriors. Golden clouds issued from his mouth. He felt helpless, as though people should take him by the arms and lead him somewhere appropriate where they would know what to do with him. He described himself humorously. He dreamed, he told me, of a clinic in Switzerland where they would bring you orange juice.

He had a doctor now, at Brigham and Women's Hospital.

He wandered silently around the room. I was sitting in the only chair.

"'Old men should be explorers'," he quoted. "'Here or there doesn't matter.'"

"What's that?" I asked, looking up at him.

"T. S. Eliot," he turned away, his face dissolving in light. "'Only a greater intensity.'"

He was like part of the air, the light. He sat entranced in the air like a dust mote.

He hung hidden like a feeling.

He thought. "So you're going to your parapsychologist," he said courteously to me. Then we both laughed. "Psychopharmacologist," I said.

He walked around the room. "The Chinese painter who, when he had finished his masterpiece, clapped his hands and disappeared into it," he reminded me with a self-deprecating smile. He was his own elaborate creation, was ready at any moment to hide in it.

"O sages standing in God's holy fire / As in the gold mosaic of a wall," I began. I said the whole thing. "I *thought* it was Yeats," he said when I had finished. "'Old men should be explorers,'" he muttered, and turned away, acting an actor acting a hundred parts at once.

I thought of a *New Yorker* cartoon from years ago, of a woman explorer confronting a very suspicious looking large animal in a jungle, and saying, "What have you done with Dr. Millmoss?" He had always reminded me of that. Is this my fate? I wondered, half-smiling. To love this because I can see it? Because he taught me to, *let* me see it this way?

I thought how a neurosis always seemed like a joke that nobody got. If we both got it, what would it be?

I partly knew.

Yet here in this environment, things were suddenly clear. I felt as though I knew him for the first time. He was de Musset, or Chopin, coughing out his life. His nervous hands, which had before seemed always stubby and still, now were everything. He had a body like everyone else's, I noticed, and a very attractive one. Before he had seemed a kind of presence, rotund with becomings. Now he looked a man most like other men, in that he was not like other men. So it was.

He was tall, and gaunt and sinewy from his illness, but his torso and his movements were strong. He seemed to relapse into the atmosphere as he stood before me. "'I am a part of all that I have met,'" he had reminded me in the beginning. He seemed indeed not to be separate from it, so that what I had known of him outside the room was an obfuscation, a demand that he be taken home.

Chapter 24

Once, at the start, I had dreamed that we moved together through total blackness, so that I could not see him, and I knew we had gone too far to go back. I was frightened, I said, "I can't do it," and then there was light, a level space opened up and we were in a cemetery with sand colored ground at the foot of a high wall from which an orange lamp shone on us. I collapsed flat on the ground by a gravestone, overcome with fear and exhaustion. "Sit down by me," I said to him, and here, among the headstones of all my dead, I said, "I want to go home."

He coughed, and moved his long fingers. I knew them now. They were the fingers of Sherlock Holmes, the fingers of an erratic, addicted violinist. They were, more than anything about him, his. They were what I had missed. There they were.

Paintings and piles of papers were beached on the floor as after a wreck. It was a Northwest Visionary School painting. Or like the Ark come to rest on Ararat. Or like monuments in the desert, Sphinx and pyramids, scarabs and votive offerings that had conducted him across to another world. Was I the slave buried with the Pharaoh? It was the room of great Egyptian stone statues in the Metropolitan where, at eleven, I had fallen in love with time and first knew what "new" meant. This place, so old, was eternally new. Like his perpetual expression of surprise, which I saw again in photographs and portraits of him at three. Here was the Little Prince on another planet, infinitely sad. Totally round eyes, covered with pointed lids now, so that the hooded, the arcane, covered new surprise, as in the pictures he spread helpless his fingers in a gesture of some new distress, and the long grimace of his three-year-old mouth remained.

I could see through myself. My faithfulness, to what I hardly knew, that was bitterly strong in me like morning coffee, tugged like a sail. I would be swept away and deposited on the pink island.

"*My* place should be this way," I said.

"It *is* like this," he murmured.

"Yours has less furniture," I answered.

"You've got a point," he said.

He was like the gilt shell of a Faberge egg.

Here we are, I thought, like a painting in a mirror.
'As idle as a painted ship / Upon a painted ocean.'
In case of fire, break glass.
Keep this door closed/
when not in use./
This may save your life/
in case of fire.
Like shouting "Fire!" in a public place.
"Fire!" he shouted.

I ran to him, was all over him, touched him, kissed him, tumbled his angelic curls. My hands were everywhere. I stepped on his feet in my eagerness to be clumsy and right. "No," I breathed. "No, no. Softly, my friend. My dear," I stopped, wrung with pity, "dear, dearest friend."

Emil had cancer of the tongue and throat. I had called a friend of my father who taught at the Harvard School of Public Health to get a doctor for a second opinion, and he told me that his daughter worked for an oncological surgeon, and to call him.

The doctor wanted to cut out Emil's tongue.

Emil was silent for about half an hour. Then he said, "*No!*"

He told me afterwards that he thought that the doctor had thought that he was in shock, but that in reality he had been listening to the spirits of his parents giving him help.

So the doctor said, "All right. We'll try chemotherapy. But it won't work."

It worked.

The doctor said it was the first time it had ever worked in a case like Emil's.

Emil had had a biopsy and months of chemotherapy at Brigham and Women's Hospital. He couldn't talk. I talked to his doctors.

I was "next of kin."

Chapter 24

I have never felt so completely alone in all my life. Before we knew he had cancer, when we were trying to find out, it was as though we were alone in Cambridge. We were so alone that it was almost romantic, as I said to Emil later. But now I was completely alone. I fielded phone calls from his friends. Emil couldn't talk. There was a great silence.

The cancer was gone for five years. It was a halcyon time for both of us. Then Emil developed cancer of the larynx. They took out his larynx.

They gave him a device, but by that time we mostly emailed each other. My father got cancer of the esophagus. Emil's emails, which I still have, are so heroic, so strengthening, so exhorting, so encouraging, and so funny, that when I read them now I find it unbelievable. He was the most capacious, deepest person I have ever known.

He was born witty. That's all he could do, be witty. All he did when he talked with the device was make jokes.

I think Emil found great peace and happiness when he couldn't talk. I didn't understand it at the time, but I do now. We had said everything we could say, and then he didn't need to talk any more. That was why, when my father got cancer, Emil could email me such cheering and encouraging and strong letters.

Then Emil got cancer of the esophagus. He had operation after operation. He emailed me from the hospital, and the rehab center, and the hospital, but when they sent him home to die he wouldn't return my emails or my letters. He couldn't be funny any more. He died without seeing me.

He died on his mother's birthday.

This meditation on my life I learned from Emil. Every morning he meditated, but it seemed to me that the essential meditation was his fingers pressing on the computer keys as he made computer art—he had a show in Paris just before he died—and sent messages to me.

I used to say to him, "Why don't you do such and such?" and he would say, "It's too external." I could see that he was right. He was completely internal, and when all he could do was press the keys of the computer, I think he had great peace.

I was able to deal with my father's cancer because I had taken care of Emil, and because of Emil's strength. But what I remember is the great triumph when his tongue and throat were cured. They had told him it wouldn't work, but he was never like anybody else. There was no one like him.

25. HIS NECK

His neck. It was cured. His neck where I kissed it. His neck where I had touched the node, had put my finger right on it. It was cured.

There had always been something *cured* about him, I thought, as though he were perpetually getting well, regenerating. The doctors called it a miracle. It didn't surprise *me*.

Everything he did was completely forgivable and totally inexplicable.

Maybe his cells were different from other people's.

His neck. Like Morse's on *Mystery*.

And the nurses had come, and the dressings had been changed, and it had stopped draining, and now there was just a scar. "I didn't ask for a scar," he said. "It will go away," I said. "No it won't," he said in surprise. "It will get fainter," I said.

"Hmm," he said.

The relief was superhuman, angelic. I felt like an ad for fabric softener. No static anywhere. Like an angel in a white gown, brimming with peace.

Absolute perfection.

Too much to bear alone.

I saw his neck before her eyes, from the back. It went with a quizzical "Hmmph?"

Dee-lighted, Monsieur.

Chapter 25

His neck. Kismet.

In other aspects of my life, I felt that I was kicking around angry fragments of exploded cannon balls. I *had* exploded, and, after explosions, peace. It was as though the guns had stopped.

I drank it in, drunk on it, couldn't get enough of the peace that was bursting my heart like a prayer.

What could I do with it? Don't knock it, I thought. This was what I had wanted.

Safe. Safe and secure.

It was the New Year. Oratorios rang out.

Beyond lay in darkness, but tonight all was glistening white.

His neck, bent a little, listening.

"Hmmph?" And the glistening, prickling silence, like snow.

Beneath the dark sky, I threw myself, coat, hat, mittens and all, backward on the white field.

The field rose up to greet me.

26. TIANANMEN SQUARE

I told Emil how everything had gone smash.

I told him that when my parents had broken up, my mother and Mistletoe and I had moved to my grandparents' apartment in New York. It was all green, with huge, forbidding family portraits with eyes that followed you. My mother told me that this was a sign of a good painting. There were bookcases fronted with glass containing rare books.

My great uncle, Henry Clay Folger, had founded the Folger Shakespeare Library in Washington. My uncle, Samuel Hemingway, had been a Shakespearean scholar and the master of Berkeley College at Yale. My uncle Frank Ellis was a professor of English at Smith, and my uncle Ignatius Mattingly was a professor of Linguistics at the University of Connecticut.

My grandfather, Edward Jordan Dimock, was a federal judge at Foley Square in New York. He had presided over the trial of Elizabeth Gurley Flynn. She had thought that he made a very fair decision, and she had sent him Christmas cards from prison.

My very beautiful grandmother, Constance Bullard, from Dedham, Massachusetts, with her long gray hair pinned up, sat in a chair all day when she had finished her wild, depressed, obdurate housework, and read Trollope. In Dedham the house where she grew up is a historic Bullard House.

They ate candied violets.

"Candied violets!" I said to Emil. "We had an acre of wild violets behind the house in Chapel Hill. It was a sacrilege. I had temper tantrums about it."

"Candied violets are considered to be a great delicacy," Emil said.

"Do you know when I lost my innocence?" I asked. "When I learned that an apple has 80 calories. I read it in a diet book. An apple! Cezanne painted apples. We had a wild apple orchard in Vermont."

Emil smiled.

My mother always referred to Reagan as "our leader." The reference was to a *New Yorker* cartoon that shows a Martian who has landed in a field of cows saying to one of them, "Take me to your leader."

My mother's sister Connie had gone to Vassar. She had been best friends with Kay Meyer, later Katharine Graham of *The Washington Post*. My mother and Connie and Kay and another friend of Connie's had gone to Europe together in the mid-30s. Connie was very radical. My mother later told me that she had learned all her politics from Connie. Connie and the other woman wanted to go to the Soviet Union. Kay's parents wouldn't let her go—one couldn't cross the border in those days. My mother remembers Connie and the other woman sitting on a flat car of a train leaving from Salzburg, with their legs hanging down, being pulled off to the Soviet Union.

My mother knew Bess Lomax, the daughter of Alan Lomax, the folk song collector, at Bryn Mawr. Once Carl Sandburg was invited to speak. There was a dinner before hand, and Bess wasn't invited. "Let's get him a bottle of Scotch," my mother said. So she and Bess had a bottle of Scotch sent up to him, with a note. When the time came for the speech, the audience waited and waited. Someone went up to Sandburg's room and came down saying, "He's drunk and walking around the room reciting his own poetry to himself." Eventually they got him down to the hall, with his guitar. He strummed for a while, and then he toward the microphone and said, *"What do we know today for sure?"* There was a shocked silence in the hall. Then Sandburg asked, "Is Bess Lomax here?"

Bess said, "Here I am, Mr. Sandburg.

"How's your father, Bess?" Sandburg said.

"Daddy's fine," Bess said.

Sandburg said, "He was always the damnedest Tory, and I was always the damnedest radical, but we were always the goddamnedest friends."

We sold the house in Vermont. My parents had bought it from my mother's philosophy professor at Bryn Mawr, Paul Weiss, $4200 for the house and 80 acres. We never went there any more and we couldn't keep it up. A doctor bought it who loved it and wanted to restore it to exactly the way it had originally been.

For a long time after we sold it, I didn't see any point in going out of the house. Cambridge had been an extension of Randolph, and without Randolph, Cambridge seemed grim and citified. I stayed home and did *Against the Vietnam War*.

One day I told Emil the worst things that had ever happened to me. We were in a restaurant. It was the day of Tiananmen Square, the student demonstration against the Chinese Communist regime. There were photos everywhere of the boy student stopping a tank by simply walking in front of it and putting up his hand. The people at the table behind Emil were talking about it. He kept smiling and leaning back to listen to them. I was glad.

I said I wished I were a Russian grandmother in Brookline with all of this behind me.

Emil said he wished he were a Russian taxi driver in New York with aspirations of being a ballet dancer.

I thought that it was like "A Star Is Born": the old drunk director teaches her everything he knows, and then he kills himself. Only I couldn't let that happen, again. Emil used to say, "How long will this last?" and I'd say, "For the duration." So I kept on until he died.

I had been so involved in my life in Cambridge that I had not seen my father and his wife and children for a number of years. But in 1991, when my mother's older sister Connie died, I went down to Princeton to see them.

27. THANKSGIVING

When I got off the train I didn't see anyone I recognized. I walked a little way down the platform and saw my father flapping his arms like a penguin as he came toward me. We hugged each other. "How are you?" he asked. "Fine!" I laughed. "I never thought I would live to see this day," he laughed because he meant it.

"I don't *believe* it!" Karen beamed and gave me a kiss. "Me, neither," I said.

"How was your trip?" my father asked.

"Fine," I said. "I had pleasant company. I sat next to a very nice man who wants me to edit his book and is coming to Cambridge to see me because I live a block from his best friend."

My father's mouth was pure joy.

On the way home we saw two deer.

The house is beautiful, built with an atrium on one side that looks out over fields and woods. It is large, and beautifully spaced. It's in the middle of trees and bushes, and seems to have its own temperature, like the air outside. It feels calm, like the fields. It could be a field among fields.

"It's so *peaceful*," I said for the third time. "It *is* peaceful," said my father. "I'm not holding up peace as the acme of human existence." "I know, I know," I murmured.

I felt as though I were on the water as I slept.

Chapter 27

The next day was Wednesday. We drove down the streets I hadn't seen since I was seven, streets I might have driven down yesterday. "These street names are so familiar to me," I said. "Olden Lane—you used to call that 'Old 'N' Lame.'" He nodded. "And I always thought that Ober Road was a funny name," I said. "Do you remember birds' nests?" I asked my father. He nodded. "They still make them." "I probably still *have* them," I cried. "Do you remember the oriole's nest next to the nursery school?" He thought, and shook his head. "It was on a high branch, the first branch. I don't know *how* you got it. You must have shimmied up the tree." My father shook his head in wonder.

The Institute appeared on the horizon like an apparition from my childhood.

We met a colleague of my father in the parking lot. I chose dish after dish of food to give me a solid sense of reality, but I was in a dream and would not awaken. "Do you remember the time I met Einstein?" I asked my father. He shook his head, trying to remember. I told him the story. "And afterwards you were terribly excited and he said to me," I concluded, turning to his colleague, "'Always remember this.'" My father smiled and shook his head. "I don't remember that," he said. "Well," I said, "among the people I went to high school with, I seem to be remembered solely as the little girl who met Einstein."

"*Really?*" cried my father in wonder.

"You look like your father," his colleague said after lunch, when my father had gone up to the library. "Around the mouth. And you have his speech rhythms."

"Mmm hmm," I said.

"Mmm hmm," my father said when we were in the car.

On Sunday we went to see an old friend of my father. "Do you think you can stay awake?" he asked on the way. "Yes," I said, "I mean, I don't know if I can stay awake, but I know I can try."

"Why, I haven't seen you since you were ten years old," Louise Morse cried. She is the widow of Marston Morse, who was at the Institute with my father. "*Seven* years old," I said. I thought she wonderful. We talked about Yeats.

"Mmm hmm," my father said when we were in the car. "Mmm *hmm.*"

We went to the Museum. I had sent my half-sister a children's book about Monet, and so my half-sister had told me to look at the Monets in the second room on the left. They are beautiful. And so are the Chaim Soutines in the first room, one of a woman like the one of the woman in the Metropolitan, my first own choice of a painting when I was a child. "They have a room in the Museum where you can sit that's all glass," my father had told me, "that looks out into trees." "*That* sounds very sensible," I said. We made our way to that room. "*This* is what we came to see," I said. "Mmm hmm," said my father.

It had been raining a little as we walked to the Museum. "Am I going too fast?" my father asked. He was holding the umbrella. My coat had a hood. "A little," I said. Walking from the Museum, my father said, "These little old ladies with bright faces. God bless 'em." I didn't know whether I felt very young or very old. There were tears in my voice all weekend. Yesterday, as I had crept into the car, feeling decrepit, my father had sung out in his rich voice, "Believe me, if all those endearing young charms."

I felt as though I had just seen them all, and I couldn't understand why we were seven years older, including myself. And it was nearly forty years since I had lived there with my father and mother, in another, littler house. So there was a foreshortening, a kind of loop the loop. The longer it was, I thought, the shorter it seemed. 'And makes me end / Where I begun.' Because I had learned everything in the meantime, I had nearly caught up to myself, and could now sit down and be in the present with everyone in the present. I had learned about youth, and about growing up, and about the tenderness of middle age and beyond, about men and about women, about needing to take care of people. "People need to be taken care of," my father had told me a long time ago. That seemed to be all there was to it.

"Daniel," I said to my tall, skinny younger half-brother, "when you lived on Long Island, one night when you were about four and you were supposed to be asleep, you came downstairs in your nightshirt to where everyone was sitting in the living room, and you said, 'Guess what I'm going to do,' and everyone said, 'What?' and you said, 'The unexpected.' And once, in the apartment in New York, when you were very young, you had all just come back from the summer, and you were lying in bed and the lights of the cars on Riverside Drive traveling along the ceiling frightened you, and you called for Daddy. And Daddy came in and you pointed to the lights and you said, 'I scared.' And Daddy said, 'So what? *I* scared. Mayor *Beame* scared. President *Ford* scared.' And you said, 'I *very* scared.' Daddy thought that was wonderful.

"And another time, Daddy called you into the living room, and he said, 'Daniel, I'd like you to meet a friend of mine. His name is Nick.' And you said, 'What his nickname?' Daddy told me all those stories. And, Seth, once Daddy was standing by your crib and he sang out, 'How sharper than a serpent's sting it is to have a toothless child.'"

My father had gotten on the phone at about that time and said, "*It's a mad scramble from start to finish!*"

When Seth was about five, I was visiting and I was reading *Henry IV Part I* for school. Seth asked me what I was reading, so I started to read to him.

"History," he murmured thoughtfully.

"This was written by William Shakespeare. Do you know who he was?" I asked.

"No," Seth said.

I said, "He was the greatest English writer."

"*No!*" Seth said.

"No?" I said.

"*No!*" Seth said. "*I'm* the greatest English writer. Give me a pencil and I'll *show* you how well I can write."

Someone had found a photograph of me and Amy, my half-sister, when Amy was four and had tacked it up on the refrigerator. Golden curls where now hung straight dark hair. "Do you remember what Amy was like as a baby?" I asked Seth. "She was so perfect, so perfectly proportioned and coordinated." "*Yes!*" said Seth. "I'd never seen such a perfect baby," I said. "She was like a ballet dancer. She had such poise, such *savoir faire*." "I remember when she first walked," round-cheeked Seth said. "We were in Washington, I think, and she was in her crib. Mom kept saying, 'Shh, don't make her nervous.' But she just walked. Amy had walked. Everyone else would follow."

"It was like having Shirley Temple around," I said. "You were a perfect little actress. You danced around all the time and entertained everybody. You were so funny, and *witty*. And so *creative*. We couldn't believe you had really done the paintings you brought home from school. The cleaning lady, Helen"—"Helen Pelegrino," said Seth thoughtfully—"kept saying, 'That one's a genius.'"

Amy laughed. "How was I funny?" she asked. "What did I say?"

"Well, let's see. When your first tooth was loose, you were in the first grade, and one of your friends had a loose tooth, too. One night your tooth came out. The next day I walked you to the bus stop, and instead of saying to your friend, 'My tooth came out,' you said, 'Did your tooth come out yet?' and she said, 'No,' and you flounced away saying, 'Then don't *bother* me with it.'"

"Ooo," said Amy. "'Don't *bother* me with it!'"

"You couldn't stop," I said. "You were like a perpetual motion machine. Daddy said, 'They forgot the stop button.' You were so perfect. Daddy said once, 'The only word I can think of to describe Amy is 'supernatural.' And you were. It was as though you had come from another planet. You were completely self-contained. You weren't affected by anything going on around you."

"I used to think it was like having a jewel," said Seth.

"Yes, it was," I said. "And everything *worked* so well. You took ballet lessons somewhere. And ice-skating. Maybe that had something to do with it."

"You were like the latest model," said Seth. "It made everything else obsolete. She was the streamlined model. I used to think she was so sophisticated. European."

Chapter 27

"Once you and Daniel were horsing around," I said, "and you were hitting each other, and I couldn't stand it, and I yelled, 'For Christ's sake, cut it out!' And Daniel, you absolutely froze, you were in shock."

"I should think so," said Daniel.

"The unthinkable had happened," I said. "I had raised my voice."

"'The unthinkable,'" Seth said thoughtfully.

"Did I really look like that picture?" Amy asked.

"Exactly," I said.

That's what had made me remember, too, but it had taken a while. They'd just grown up, that was all. But all the rest had really happened, and it was terribly important.

"Amy and I have to show you how we can play and sing 'Send in the Clowns,'" I announced to my father. My voice as I sang was rich and strange. When I finished I turned around and my father was wiping his eyes. "Happy-sad," he said, and then, "Life is corny."

I picked up a guitar that lay on the sofa and tried it. My father tuned it and I played the guitar, all my father's old songs, and all my tears overflowed, and I sang beyond the tears.

I sang every song he had ever sung, or heard, and every song I knew. I sang Joan Baez, Cole Porter, Rodgers and Hart, Woody Guthrie, Livingston Taylor, union songs, cowboy songs, Marlene Dietrich, children's songs that had been on the first black record he had ever given me. I sang "West Side Story." I recited Whitman's "On the beach at night stands a child with her father, / Watching the East, the evening sky / . . . .Weep not, child, weep not, father. / The Pleiades will again shine. . . ."

My father had given me two guitars. He had played the guitar after the divorce, when he was living in one room on East 81st Street.

He sat on the sofa with his back to me. Karen listened for a while, and then she went into the kitchen.

Finally I put down the guitar and went into the kitchen.

"You're very good," Karen said.

Thanksgiving

After a while she went into the living room to check on my father. When he finally came into the kitchen, I could see that he had been crying and crying.

He smiled and nodded.

"Gee," he said. "I only know about three chords."

"I have to prepare my Monday lecture on Sunday night, and my Tuesday lecture on Monday night, and my Thursday lecture on Wednesday night," said my father in a kind of continual amazement. He had been asked to start an Institute of Biostatistics at Rutgers. "Mmm hmm," I said. "Ah, well," he said, "that will soon be over." "But think," I said, "if you didn't lecture *them*, someone would lecture *you*." "I wouldn't mind that," he said, wandering into the kitchen. "I wouldn't mind that at all."

"I've had such a wonderful va*ca*tion," I said. "Why?" he asked. "Someone else doing the shopping, and the cooking, and the driving," I said. "It's like a ho*tel*." "Well, that's what it's meant to be like," he said. "I hope someone will be doing all of that for *me* soon." "It's *nice*," I said.

"Maybe I'll go out to Seattle for Christmas and see Mummy," I said. "Now that I can fly." "You can fly?" he asked. "I can fly," I said, waving my arms. This had been my first train ride in twenty years. He laughed. "I can't fly," he said. "I wish I could, but I can't." "But you can teach other people," I said. He smiled and nodded. "Those who can't do, teach," I said. He nodded.

"Go for a bike ride. Take my bike," Karen said. I rode down the driveway, turned right, rode to the end of the street, and came back. Karen was on the phone. I made a V sign. "Works." Karen nodded.

When I had been having trouble with pottery, my father had said, "I tried to throw a pot on the wheel once." "What happened?" I asked. There was a pause. "Didn't work."

"I went for a bike ride," I told my father. "Really?" he exclaimed. "On Karen's bike?" "Yes," I said. "Karen's bike is perfect for me." "Really?" he cried in joy.

Chapter 27

Seventeen people sat down to Thanksgiving dinner. I couldn't sort out the neighbors. I kept falling asleep. Then Karen changed seats with me, and I sat next to my father. "My eyes itch," my father said, rubbing them. "Maybe it's my smoking," I said. "I'm not smoking very much." "I've noticed," he said. "You start them and then you put them out." "That's why I keep falling asleep," I gave a little rebellious tug, "but I'm *here*." My father's eyes glowed. He *was* like Jeremy Brett as Sherlock Holmes.

"What sort of books do you write?" asked the man seated on my other side. "Autobiography," my father told him. "She's had a full, rich life." "I wrote to someone recently something I thought sounded interesting," I said. "I said, 'Writing—the point of writing is to remember; the point of painting is to forget.'" "Well, that sounds very good, but you— " my father started with relish. "*You* have a verbal tick that won't stop!" I cried. He smiled. "I *know*. I'm a *painter*. No, it's true," I went on. "In writing, you have to remember how *you* felt," he nodded, "and how *she* looked," he nodded, "and why *they* behaved the way they did," he nodded, "but in painting you have to turn all that off, and go into something called your unconscious," he nodded, "and think about light," he nodded, "and paint," he nodded, "and color, and be in the present."

When I returned to Cambridge, I was still in a dream. It lasted for days. It snowed.

I was beginning to awaken from the dream when I spoke to my father on the phone.

"I bought a futon like a cloud and contact lenses with the money you gave me," I said.

"Had you ever had them?" he asked. "Yes, but they were a nuisance. You had to bake them." "*Bake* them?" he said. "Yes, in a little kit, every time you took them out. But now you don't have to." "Yah, get yourself fixed up," he said. I thought of the funny little figure I had felt myself to be.

"What about Terry Anderson?" I said. He had been held hostage for seven years and had just been released.

"Oh," he said, "he seems in great shape."

"How did they *do* it?" I asked. "Mmm hmm," he said. "It's like being in a wet suit under water for seven years, and then emerging." "Mmm, hmm," he said. "I think *I* do nothing," I said. "Mmm hmm," he said. "I sort of feel like him," I confessed. "Mmm hmm," he said.

"I had a lovely time," I said.

"Good," he said.

I broke into the dream. "I wrote a story about it. Every word is there."

"Every word of *what*?" he said.

"Every word of every conversation," I said. He made a sound of amazement. "I have a tape memory," I said, "which is getting shorter and shorter. For three days I remembered every word of every conversation, so I wrote a story. I used to be able to remember conversations from ten years ago verbatim. I don't know why I didn't just write a whole lot of novels. It never occurred to me. But I'll send it to you. Then you'll have it all captured in deathless prose."

"Do!" he exclaimed. "Like carving a statue. The point is what to leave out."

"That's right," I said. "I had to leave things out. It was getting too long. I do that when I edit people's books. I cut out two chapters, and there's a great book." "Mmm *hmm*," he said. "You could do that with people's lives," I said. "Just leave in the day they were born, and their childhood birthdays, and their wedding day, and their fiftieth anniversary." He made a sound of sympathy. "You'd have a great life."

"You could do it with the telephone book," he said. "Or world history."

"That's right," I said. "Okay, I'll send it to you as soon as I get the quotation marks straightened out."

"Do that!" he said, delighted.

"When you see it, you'll remember it," I said.

He laughed.

Chapter 27

When my father died, I moved out of my mother's apartment on Shepard Street. It was like an archeological dig: all my paintings and paints and art table on the surface, and below them layers of books of my family's, and ancient trunks of lace and linen of my great grandmother's, and my mother's paintings, and all my clothes and Mistletoe's clothes going back to the 1950s, and bedspreads everywhere.

Mom's Moving moved in and divided the apartment into sections and closets like brain surgeons, and went to work. I sat on the bed and every china animal, every bead, was brought to me for consideration.

My mother's jewelry, jewelry she had given me from 8th street in Greenwich Village when we lived in New York, Mistletoe's high school text books, perfume and cologne, Rose Geranium bath powder, a wicker basket of blankets, the bathing suit Sylvia taught me to swim in when I was seven on Fisher's Island—a huge shingled house with a croquet lawn and a path of wild roses leading to snail covered rocks and the sea, and I actually did learn to swim, Sylvia saying, "I won't let go until you're ready," and my saying, "Okay, let go," and I was *swimming*, so exciting, and the upstairs bedroom where I read in bed all day, *Judith and Jane* and *Four Margarets* and all the sequels, while the fog horn sounded outside the window—papers, all my papers, Emil's papers, stuffed animals, teddy bears and koalas given to me and Mistletoe by my father in a paper bag straight from Australia, which we named, because they looked like Einstein, Professor Theophilus Bush and Dr. Bush Kobear—tables, lamps, Canton China, Victorian carved chairs—all these things it was a necessity to decide about. I had two antiques dealers in, and one of them, Duncan Wells Purdy, had a gallery attached to his shop. He walked into the living room, which was completely filled with my paintings and my prints, and "discovered" me.

"Can I be your agent?" he asked.

"*Yes*," I said.

So lots of paintings and prints went off to his gallery.

It was so painful seeing our childhood clothes pass by in boxes for the Salvation Army. I caught sight of a pair of plaid shorts, and I couldn't look any more.

I had a large collection of rare books from my mother's uncle, Henry Clay Folger, first editions of Hawthorne and Emerson, Coleridge, and a lot more. They covered the top of the upright piano we had given to my father for his birthday in Chapel Hill. "*Sell them*," my father had said about the books. So I called the Brattle Bookstore and the owner came and bought them and everything else I wanted to go—everything but my mother's art books and all the poetry, *The Home Book of Verse*, and all the Oxford editions that we had always had, and all my poetry books, and my political books, and *all* the books my father gave me, and a lot else.

"Put it out on the *street*," my father had said about the upright piano. So I traded it with the movers for a spinet.

Mom's Moving was heaven, so skillful, so tactful, so loving. It took about six months.

At the end, when everything was in boxes and there was nothing left to do, I found a pen and paper and wrote to Richard Wilbur, sending him my poetry manuscript, which I had always wanted to do. He was in my mind when I wrote so much of it.

He wrote me a letter, saying, ". . . I have enjoyed sampling your poems . . . which have the freshness and surprise that come of finding out exactly what one feels or means, and which can be as electrically simple as the song on p. 54. Many good wishes to you."

    song

    lovers come and go
    under the trees
    together and apart
    that's how it is
    love goes
    the old ardor stays
    joy lasts a day

Chapter 27

love lasts forever

lovers leave
leaving the old love grieving
joy departs
pain remains
pain and joy remain
lovers are always leaving
all lovers go
love, all love, love, stays

I wrote back to him thanking him for his letter and saying that it was the culmination of my life. He wrote back that he was glad that he had made me happy.

Richard Wilbur and Leonard Bernstein—*Candide*, and *West Side Story*. Leonard Bernstein's doctor advised him to retire, he announced his retirement, and the next day he died.

"What do you think of that?" asked my father,

"Never retire!" I said.

My father retired at 84, and immediately got the cancer that killed him.

Charles Schulz, the creator of *Peanuts*, died as his announced last strip was going to press.

My new apartment, tiny, has huge windows. It is two blocks from the building where my father roomed when he was in graduate school at Harvard. It has pine trees and maple trees all around it, and rose bushes, and an iris garden, and a lilac bush. It is like Vermont, and Chapel Hill, and Princeton, and where I taught, and Shepard Street, only things are very clear.

28. STAUGHTON LYND AND HOWARD ZINN

When Bill Clinton first ran for president, for me it was like enlightenment. Here was a Democrat, after all those years of Reagan and George Bush, someone my age, of my generation, the Vietnam generation, who might be in power. I edited my book, *Against the Vietnam War*, a collection of essays by, among others, Noam Chomsky, Staughton Lynd, Howard Zinn, Carl Oglesby, Joan Baez, Dave Dellinger, David Harris, Martin Luther King, Jr., Bill Ayers, David Cortright, other Vietnam veterans, and less well known people who had been active in the antiwar movement.

My colleagues, the contributors to the book, especially Staughton Lynd and Howard Zinn, have remained my colleagues and close associates. My interest in political issues became at that point very clear and intense, and it has only become more so.

I would never have done the book if it hadn't been for Jeff. He brought the whole thing so close.

Carl Oglesby had been the last person I saw before I left teaching. He had been the head of Students for a Democratic Society—SDS. He was at the college for a semester. No one in my department had ever mentioned the war in Vietnam in the entire time I was there, from 1973 to 1976. It had ended in 1975. I thought as I left, "Why can't I have a political life?"

So when I decided to do a book about the Vietnam War, the first person I called was Carl. He was living in Cambridge. We talked, and he told me to call Staughton Lynd. Staughton had been one of the leaders of the anti-Vietnam War movement. Carl said, "Staughton Lynd is a prince on earth."

I really wasn't sure I could deal with anyone so virtuous. I called about a hundred other people, including all those who became contributors to the book. And finally, I called Staughton Lynd.

I told him what I was doing and how I had come to think of doing it.

He listened attentively—he is the best listener I have ever known, and he must have been the most wonderful teacher—and then he said, "Susannah, that's a very moving story. I think you should write the introduction about that."

So I wrote the introduction, beginning with:

> At my Harvard twenty-fifth reunion in 1992, there was a symposium entitled "Vietnam: The Choices We Made." As the panelists spoke, some people wept in silence. It was like a memorial service. After the panelists had spoken, lines of people stood at the microphones placed around the room, waiting in silence to tell their own stories. Each person struggled to bear witness to a long nightmare, hitherto unspoken, unshared. The shaking backs of friends and strangers signified what they held—and held in—in common. "We never talked about it," some said afterwards.
>
> In Harvard Square it seemed that the sidewalk was glass, that below it lay the rubble of the Vietnam War on which American society was built, and that no one was looking down.
>
> So, I would look down. I would not deny it any longer. I would look at the war and the antiwar movement, so inextricable.

I collected all the essays, and I had no idea how to put them in order. Staughton wrote a table of contents.

My publisher, Syracuse University Press, said I needed an index.

Staughton wrote the index.

I told Staughton that I wanted to put a poem of mine in the introduction, but that my father didn't think I should promote myself that way.

"Susannah," said Staughton, "how old are you?"

I sent Staughton the poem. He said that he liked it—he understood it very well—and that he thought that I should put it in the introduction.

H. Bruce Franklin, who had been very active in the antiwar movement and had published several books on the subject, helped me with the rest of the introduction. So I had an introduction, a table of contents, and Staughton wrote a conclusion.

I said to Staughton, "Without you there would be no *book*. Just a lot of pieces of paper."

Staughton and Howard Zinn helped me select the essays and with all the editorial business. I wanted to include some poems of Daniel Berrigan that were out of print. Howard brought me his copy of *Night Flight to Hanoi*.

I was in my bathrobe dealing with the copy editors when he arrived. He came in. The living room was completely filled with my paintings. Howard admired them. He told me that his wife was an artist.

I had a huge cardboard graph titled "The Input/Output System of the United States Economy" which I had picked up from someone's trash and used as an easel to which I taped my canvases. The area around where the canvases had been was splashed with paint. My father had seen it and thought that it was terribly funny, so it had become a work of art in its own right. Howard loved it.

I showed him a painting of my house at the college where I had taught. He was surprised. I told him that I had left, that I hadn't liked academia. He agreed. He told me that he had decided to retire from B.U., and that he thought that I had done the right thing.

I worked very closely with Howard all through the publication process.

The book, *Against the Vietnam War: Writings By Activists*, came out before my father died. I had been afraid that it wouldn't.

Chapter 28

Staughton and I had great communion when we were working on the book. I talked to him on the phone in Niles, Ohio. Once I said something to him and he said, "Well, Susannah, this is the 1960s, isn't it?"

In the 1960s and 1970s, when you talked something out straight, it was called "making revolution."

I showed an early draft of this memoir and my manuscript of poems, "Eclipse of the Moon," to Howard. He was extremely gracious and encouraging and helpful.

When my father was dying, I called Staughton.

September 11, 2001 came just after I had moved and was dealing with my father's estate. I talked to Staughton about collecting essays from some of the contributors to *Against the Vietnam War* on the subject of 9/11 and after sending them to magazines. It developed into *Peace Not Terror*.

My mother continued to be a great solver of editorial problems.

29. PEACE

Jeff and I were sitting in bed, in 1986.

"In Vietnam once I was told to go down in a tunnel, alone, and kill anyone that I saw. I went down, and there was this guy, in black pajamas, like they wore, asleep. And I shot him through the head."

Jeff was crying and shaking. I held him.

"It's all right," I said. "It's over."

Jeff had gone to jail for shoplifting when he was a teenager, during the war, and they had given him a choice of jail or going into the army. They said he would go to Germany. He chose the army, and over international waters the pilot got on the intercom and said, "The orders have been changed. We're going to Vietnam."

Jeff had been a sergeant when he was ordered to take his troops into a village. They retreated with a third of them lost. He was ordered to take them in again, and again they retreated with another third of them lost. He was ordered to take them in again, and he refused. He was given a dishonorable discharge and sent home. He joined Vietnam Veterans Against the War.

He was my age. He had worked in a library for a while, and then had been a roadie for Elvis for three years. He had been married four times, had a dead child, a baby who was taken away from him by the state, and a five-year-old daughter whom he worshipped.

Chapter 29

He spent all his time reading in restaurants. He told me that once in a coffee shop, he had gotten into a conversation with a Harvard professor for an hour, and at the end of it the professor had asked him, "What department are you in?"

Jeff said, "I'm a street person."

He told me about working for Elvis. He said that when he first arrived at Graceland he was taken into a room to meet Elvis. The room was covered in fur and Elvis was sitting in a chair. He said hello to Jeff. Jeff said that there was something about his presence that was indescribable. That night he couldn't sleep for thinking about Elvis. He wanted to *do* something for him. Jeff was like that. So he got up in the middle of the night and vacuumed the rug outside Elvis's room, over and over.

Jeff told me he had slept with 300 women when he was a roadie for Elvis. It was part of the job. All of the women would go crazy about everyone around Elvis. Jeff was married at the time, and on tour a lot, and he said he and his wife had an understanding about it.

He talked to me about Colonel Parker, Elvis's manager, and about the day Elvis died. He said that he was waiting in Maine with Colonel Parker and a lot of other people for Elvis to arrive for a performance. It was raining, and it got later and later, and Elvis didn't show up, and finally they got a phone call that he had died.

"You should write a book," I kept telling him. "You've been hit by every social and political current in the United States."

One night Jeff had been at Joy of Movement, the dance studio, with some friends, and, as he turned to leave, he suddenly turned back to see that a girl had jumped out of a window. Without knowing how he did it he raced back and pulled her up by the collar.

"She was light as a feather," he said.

Jeff was a miracle.

"I don't question it," he said.

But underneath there was a terrific current of agitation and tension.

One morning we got up early and I walked with him to the Science Center. He waved goodbye and vanished in the mist.
He was my freedom, and he went to jail.

He told me that his mother had tried to drown him. He said, "My mother was a very intelligent—drunk."
His uncle had been a hobo, and he used to take Jeff down under the bridge where he and his friends slept and they would have a fire and tell stories.

One night before he was to take off for California we watched the last game of the World Series. The Red Sox lost. "It would have been too much," I said, "if they had won and you went to California tomorrow." In the morning I walked with him to the subway, and then I cried and cried. One of his friends, a street person, was very nice. "Oh, he's wonderful," he said.

But he always came back.

I had a job working in the office of the Unitarian Church on Church Street. One morning I got up and I felt as if something awful had happened, some tragedy. I thought I couldn't go to work. Finally I got there about two hours late. "Oh," I burst out to my supervisor, "a friend of mine was hit by a car and killed on Linnaean Street."
I didn't know why I said it. I was terribly upset. It was Christmas time and my supervisor was very nice; we just decorated the tree, we didn't work that day.
A couple of days later I got a call from Jeff. He was in the hospital. He'd been hit by a car in Harvard Square. He was very badly injured. He said that someone who'd seen the accident said that Jeff had gone flying through the air like a rag doll.

Chapter 29

In bed with him, I used to put my head on his chest and cry and cry, or just go to sleep. I felt safer when I was with him than I had ever felt in my life.

Once I told him that he had said to me, "You sleep. I'll stand guard."

"Did I *really* say that?" he asked.

At one point he was living in a shelter and planning to leave for Maine. We both knew that there was no way it could work out. I didn't hear from him for a couple of weeks. Finally he came over.

"I can't stand this," I said. I thought, I'm never having another relationship. This is too hard.

"I can't either," he said. "That's why I've been withdrawing."

But he always came back.

I had known Jeff for about 14 years. He would come and go. He would spend a couple of nights with me, and then he would say, "I'm getting soft! I have to get back on the street!" He was so shell shocked from Vietnam that he couldn't live in an apartment. I made him get one once, and he left in a day. He could only live on the street.

I would send him to California to see relatives of mine I thought he would like, and he would come back. He would go to see his daughter in Connecticut, and he would come back. He would decide to just get on a bus, for anywhere, and he would come back. He went on the lam when the police were looking for him after he hit a guy with a bottle, and he came back.

He had an unerring instinct for coming back at the wrong time. I was so deeply involved with Emil and Emil's cancer, and Jeff kept coming back, like a cat. He was very faithful and loyal, but he had sort of gone wild. The first time we came into the apartment he made straight for the refrigerator. Nothing was his, and everything. He showed me a fork and spoon that he carried with him that Rikki had given to him. He was like a kid running away from home.

All of these relationships had a sort of dreamlike quality because most of the time I was alone.

Emil and I had walked to Harvard Square during the 1991 Gulf War. All the stores had their doors and windows open and their radios blaring, like loud speakers. Emil and I were on opposite sides about the war, as we were about Vietnam. I didn't care.

The radios sounded so loud, like all the pain and anger I'd ever known.

My father was very practical. "Think of all that prickly heat!" he said. "Well," he said, "I think it's good. People worry about their health too much."

Jeff's friends got him drunk and he got in a fight and he nearly killed the guy who attacked him, with a bottle.

He told me had done it reflexively. "That's what they taught us to do in the army," he told me.

He went to jail for two years, and the day he got out he arrived at my door. I was sort of expecting him, but he was different. I could tell that he was violent.

He showed me a picture some other prisoner had drawn, of me.

I was shaking like mad. I was in my nightgown.

"I can't deal with this right now," I said. "I'm going to kick you out."

"Okay," he said. He went to the door. He kissed me on the cheek, and he bit me, hard.

"We'll be in touch," he said.

It took me a few days to get over being so glad to see him and to begin to feel that jail had murdered him. And that he wouldn't come back.

I had a lot of remorse toward Jeff. He left and came back to find that I was seeing Emil. And now he was gone.

I hoped he got on a bus out of there.

I hoped he didn't jump off a roof, like Rikki. That's all. Yeats says, 'A pity beyound all telling / Is hid in the heart of love.' You love people with your soul, and you are so afraid for them. All the violence and waste, caring and harm.

After about ten years, and after thinking very hard all of Memorial Day weekend in 2006, I knew exactly where Jeff was. His daughter Aubrey, whom he had worshipped, lived in Connecticut. I called Connecticut information and I got his number.

He's married, living in a very nice apartment, and he's, as he says, "domesticated." He owns things for the first time. All of Elvis's CDs, all the Beatles CDs. He has an orange cat. He sounds exactly the same, only very comfortable.

All over the world people marched in the streets against another war.

September 11 did it for everyone—we'd all had enough war.

It was like a flowering. It was as though everyone all over the world had just flowered.

The press compared it to the revolutions of 1848.

It was like 1968, but better.

We had a blizzard, which, they say, was greater than the blizzard of '78.

After the blizzard of '78 there was no traffic, no noise. People skied down Massachusetts Avenue in peace. And then we sat and watched the army roll in. But there was no looting, no chaos. People breathed fresh air.

Eisenhower said that people want peace so much that sooner or later governments will have to get out of the way and let them have it.

30. HOME

The apple trees that had gone wild in our orchard in Vermont reminded me of my mother's hair. I was called Nanaberrybush. I had called myself Nana when I was little and one of my great aunts assured us that in Australia there was a bush called a nanaberry bush. So that was I. Sometimes I was just called Berrybush. There were berry bushes all over the property in Vermont; we considered them the chief asset, and spent days assiduously picking into coffee cans and sauce pans, and in the evening making raspberry jam and jelly with Sure-Jell, skimming away the froth with a long handled wooden spoon and sealing the jars with paraffin. We also had black raspberries, outside the front door and up on top of the hill as well. These were the rarest, and my favorites. And blackberries, but these ripened later, after our greatest conserving efforts had passed. We brought back every fall more sun-filled memories than we could ever eat. We spent the summer storing up the summer to take back to New York in September. There was always a sadness about summers in Vermont: sadness that they would not last forever, and a sadness at not knowing what to do with the riches. We made them into jam.

My mother would stand in the kitchen by the hour, smoking and dreaming. But she was happiest when a practical catastrophe hit and she had to "fly into action." She was always flying into action. The cellar wall made of stones collapsed, and she had to call a man with a backhoe to level the ground so that a new cement wall could be poured. She was out there, talking to the man with the backhoe, and she was completely in charge, completely happy, in her blue jeans that were worn in front from hours of washing dishes at the huge limestone kitchen sink. The night the chimney of the great wood stove caught fire, long after we children were asleep, and she had to stay up all night watching it before she could get someone to come in the morning and put it out, was the most exciting night of her life. She prowled around after we were in bed, checking on this and that, holding the screen door open so that she could look at the stars, and she was the master, this was her ship, she was the captain of her soul.

My mother loved to drive. She was at ease at the wheel. She would say, "Shall we go for 'pin? Shall we go the long way round?" and we would drive along the small Vermont highways, looking out at the insurmountably beautiful fields and hills and weather, the hot breeze blowing in our faces, blowing our hair till it looked like birds' nests. One summer when she was working she drove us from New York up to Vermont every Friday night and back every Sunday night, nine hours each way with stops for carsickness and hamburgers and gift shops that we plundered each time as if they were something completely new. Slowing down into the traffic coming into New York at the end of the weekend, we would wake up to the smell of exhaust and the smell of New York and the muggy air, and the old buildings, and the lights, and we would feel as though we were waking from a wild, free dream into the sure, steady, slowly moving, comforting, complete familiarity which was the exit into 79th Street, and home. We loved coming back. The city at night was peace, was rest, after the vibrating, swiftly moving weekend.

Such peace as we turned into 79th Street.

Printed in Great Britain
by Amazon